RISE

THE ORDINARY

THE LIFE BEHIND HER SMILE

Lakisha P Hunter

RISE ABOVE THE ORDINARY: The Life Behind Her Smile

KDC Publishing
kdcpublishingllc@gmail.com
www.isoarworldwide.com/kdc-publishing

© 2024 Lakisha P Hunter

All rights reserved solely by the author. The author guarantees all contents are original and do not infringe upon the legal rights of any other person or work. No part of this book may be reproduced in any form without the permission of the author. The views expressed in this book are not necessarily those of the publisher.

Reproduction or translation of any part of this book beyond that permitted by Section 107 or 108 of the 1976 United States Copyright Act without permission of the copyright owner is unlawful. Requests for permission or more information should be directed to:

Lakisha P Hunter
lphunter@rise-above-the-ordinary.org
1rato.org

Unless otherwise indicated, Scripture quotations are taken from the King James Version (KJV) – *public domain.*

Printed in the United States of America

Paperback ISBN-13: **978-0-9858526-1-0**

LAKISHA P HUNTER

WHAT OTHERS ARE SAYING

Death was assigned to this woman of God to destroy her identity and destiny. But, God spoke and said, "Not So! She shall live and not die, to declare, decree and establish My work! And it is so." Lakisha Hunter has persevered, survived, and triumphantly conquered her tests, trials, and tribulations, and has risen victorious.
~ Pastor Dr. Jeanette Sams

There are a lot of memoirs out there to be read; however, to be transparent with no holds barred to tell your life journey challenges with raw and grit is an unforgettable story with a purpose. A fascinating page-turner is on the horizon with The Life Behind Her Smile! Lakisha Hunter is an influential writer who succeeds on her terms with this riveting, raw, and gritty story of her life unplugged. She will keep the reader engaged and moving along in her journey, sharing her unpredictable past of how she was

RISE ABOVE THE ORDINARY: The Life Behind Her Smile

raised, caring for her siblings, and surviving street life to becoming Chef K and giving back to others. If you've never had hope and didn't believe that better is coming, this is an inspiring story of how prayer changes things and how God was entwined into Lakisha's life from the beginning so that she could be an example for countless others. I highly recommend this novel to you.

~ Brenda McCain
Author: Walking Upright: Order My Steps
Radio Host: Let's Stay Together Talk Show
Theatre Critic: Let's Play Theatrical Reviews
Blogger: Club Fifty
Graphic Designer: eFay-Designs

The Life Behind Her Smile is engrossing, skillfully weaving together heartbreak, obstacles, triumph, defeat, and victory in moments that you will remember, relate to, and be inspired to dream again! In the face of challenges that seek to define and diminish you, it inspires you to believe again. Author Lakisha Hunter helps us realize that failure is not defeat, and our valleys don't prevent us from having mountaintop experiences. Reading The Life Behind Her Smile is highly recommended as it contains a blueprint that has the power to transform our lives and love us from pain to promise.

~ Bishop Tommie L. Triplett, Jr.

TABLE OF CONTENTS

Chapter 1 In The Beginning.................11

Chapter 2 Ready For School 25

Chapter 3 School Of Hard Knocks.................39

Chapter 4 Hard Knocks Get Harder.................53

Chapter 5 The Rise Begins.................69

Chapter 6 The Rise Makes Changes.................83

Chapter 7 Changes Bring Better Days.................99

Chapter 8 Turns And Shifts For Better.................117

Chapter 9 Yet Life Keeps Life'N.................137

Chapter 10 I Made It In Spite Of 157

Chapter 11 A Love Like Daddy's.................171

Chapter 12 Trust You, Not They.................199

Chapter 13 Life's Most Important Seek.................223

Chapter 14 Home Sweet PFOM Home.................249

RISE ABOVE THE ORDINARY: The Life Behind Her Smile

Chapter 15 And In My Closing..........................271

Thank Yous..291

Dedication............…................................295

CHAPTER 1

An attack is usually unexpected except to the attacker, *but what's unexpected to the attacker is your expected end*!
LPH

LAKISHA P HUNTER

IN THE BEGINNING

RISE ABOVE THE ORDINARY: The Life Behind Her Smile

IN THE BEGINNING

I remember being told of an experience where death tried to take me at the age of 2.

My mother gave birth to my older brother Michael at the tender age of 14. My father, who was 21 at the time, married my mother who was 17.

My mom and dad lived above Paynes Tavern on 43rd Street where my mother's mom worked.

While living on the Second floor over the tavern, I was found and about to fall out of the second-floor bedroom window.

At some point, people outside the lounge saw that this baby (me) was about to fall out of this Window.

A man by the name of Munchie, who was intoxicated at the time, saw me and positioned himself to catch me if I was to fall.

He was nervous and sweating bullets, I heard.

My mom came into the room and saw me in the open window.

While trying not to startle me, she was gentle and careful so that I wouldn't fall.

As she reached for me, I fell out the window with Munchie positioned below…Aaaaaaaaand,…..He Caught me!

Next thing I know, I'm 5 years old and living in the projects on 43rd and State Street in Chicago.

I remember living on the 8th floor with my mom, brother, stepfather, and my stepfather's family.

There were a *lot of people* living in this apartment.

I'm not sure how long I lived there, but it seemed like a long time. But I don't remember seeing my mom or dad any more than twice while living there.

I remember one night my mom came into the room where my brother and I were sleeping. She woke me up to tell me to come to the front of the apartment to open my toys: it was Christmas!

Later that same day, my father came over to visit. I don't remember seeing him before now either; but somehow, I knew him and his presence.

I remember feeling so warm and safe in his arms. This feeling was different from when my mother would hold me. I actually felt more connected to him.

I remember him putting me to sleep that night. But I also remember waking up because I was cold.

I woke up noticing that I wasn't in my father's arms anymore. Then, I immediately became scared because I thought he was gone.

I rushed out of bed and ran to the front. And, to my surprise, sitting in the corner in a chair was my father.

He jumped because I startled him.

He signaled for me to come to him, so I did anxiously.

"What you doin' up?" he whispered. I don't remember saying anything though.

I started to climb into his lap, but he pushed me away. He said, "No, baby. Daddy don't smell too good." [He reeked of wine and cigarette smoke. My father was an alcoholic.] "Daddy don't want you smellin' like him."

I remember crying and struggling with him to sit in his lap until he gave up and picked me up into his arms.

See, I didn't care what he smelled like. To me, my father smelled like *Old Spice*! And besides, I was safe and warm again!

I don't remember seeing my father again after this until I was 7 years old.

Now, I have a younger sister named Falisha, but we call her *May-May*. She's two years younger than me. We didn't have the same father, but we were close.

Although no one told me to, I felt like I had to protect her for some reason.

My big brother Michael was always either in school or in the streets hustling. And he stayed at my grandfather's (mother's father) house a lot.

He was crazy about my grandfather; and so was I.

I loved to visit my grandmother though (my father's mother). I was her only grandchild. She loved me, and so did my aunts and uncles.

While I was with my grandmother, I felt safe – just like I did with my father.

I don't know why I never felt this way at home though. Home was always dark and gloomy to me.

Young Intuition

For some reason, I knew that me, my sister, and brother didn't have much. Maybe I knew this because I saw the way everyone else around us dressed, and I heard what they would say as we walked past.

I remember having to wear the clothes and shoes my stepcousins didn't want. And I would hear them, as well as other kids down the porch, sometimes laugh and talk about us.

But it didn't matter to us. We thought the clothes were new! And they *were*… to us.

At my grandma Burneda's house (my father's mother), I had plenty of clothes - *brand new* – for me and only me!

Whenever I would come over to spend the weekend, my grandmother would give me a bath, wash and comb my hair, and put me on my favorite "Wonder Woman" undies.

This was big to me because I don't remember ever taking a bath at home.

At my grandma Burneda's, I had all the food I wanted to eat. I loved being at my grandmother's, but I never wanted to stay longer than a weekend because I didn't want to be without my sister.

Sometimes she would come over to my grandmother's house with me. But May-May *loved* to be under my mother. So, she didn't come with me most of the time.

I remember telling my grandmother what those kids would say to me about having to wear hand-me-downs. So, she allowed me to take most of my clothes and shoes home. But she stopped letting me take clothes and shoes home when she noticed that the clothes weren't coming back with me on the weekends.

The clothes and shoes weren't coming back because my mother would have sold them all on the streets for money or drugs before I could get back to my grandmother's house to bring the clothes back.

If anyone was to describe me as a child, I was a very angry kid who didn't talk much. I wasn't disrespectful but didn't like being bothered by people. I was told I was always too serious as a child.

I remember my grandma Burneda asking me if I was in school yet. When I told her I wasn't in school, I could tell by her facial expression that she was upset at my response. So, I began to cry.

My grandmother, seeing that I was sad, quickly told me, "Aww baby, you did nothing wrong. You can always tell me anything!"

I asked, "Why did you look mad?"

She laughed and said, "Oh, nothing."

Moments later, I heard my grandmother on the telephone cussing at someone, asking "Why the *?!^ ain't my grandbaby in school?!!....I'm TI'RED o' talkin'!...I'm gone TAKE her from you!!!"

At that point, I knew she was talking to my mother.

I felt so bad. So, I decided not to tell my grandmother anything else that would make her mad at my mother...I felt that I was responsible for my grandmother being upset with my mother.

Daddy's Home Again

I'm not sure if my grandmother talked to my father about me not being in school, or if it was just a coincidence. But he stopped by days later after two years of not seeing him at all.

I remember running into his arms and hugging him so tight. I was so full of excitement that I almost knocked him over.

But he didn't almost fall because I rushed him. He almost fell because he was drunk.

Anyway…

Once again, I remember waking up and wondering if he was gone. I prayed that he wasn't.

Suddenly, I heard his voice and ran to the front where he and my mother were arguing about me not going to school. When my dad noticed me there listening to them argue, he told me to come and sit with him.

Once again smelling like that good ole *Old Spice* (but, Not).

He asked, "Do you know how to spell your name?"

I said, "No."

He took me to the kitchen table and sat me in a chair as he stacked some crates next to me for himself to sit on. He pulled a brown paper bag from under his shirt and sat it on the table.

Inside the brown bag was his drink (Night Train). He took the bottle out of the bag and ripped the bag open. He got a knife from out of the kitchen drawer to sharpen a stub of a pencil.

He then wrote my first, last, and middle name across the ripped brown paper bag.

He said, "I'm only going to show you a few times. Then, you have to do it yourself without my help."

Breath reeking with alcohol and all, He put the pencil in my right hand and guided my hand across the paper bag. He then told me to repeat after him as we wrote my name.

"LAKISHA…PETRICE…HUNTER." (sounding out the letters and the spelling of my name)

Before the night was over, I knew how to spell and write my name!

He said to my brother, "Help her (me) learn everything you [have] learned in school." Then, turning to me he said, "When he sits down to do his homework, you sit with him until he's finished."

As a child, I always did what I was told because I didn't like people to be upset with me.

Starting School

It had to have been September when my mother put me in school for the first time. I turned 8 years old in October.

I carved a pumpkin in school in November and played in the snow for recess in December.

At this time, my mom had two more children: Twins - Stephanie and Steven. They were two years old, and she was pregnant with one on the way. This new baby will be Danielle who we call Nikki.

But I don't remember seeing much of my mother at this time either. She was with a man named Chuck, according to my angry stepfather who was stuck with five children.

Not only did I miss my mom, but I missed school as well.

Now, we were living with my mother's friend Lisa, who was a drunk. And I could not *stand* her.

She would beat her kids with anything she could get her hands on. So, I was terrified!

I prayed, kept my sisters and brothers close, and made sure they didn't get in her way.

Not Me And Mine

Lisa had a son, and he would look at May-May in such a *weird* way…a way that a man shouldn't look at a little girl.

I can't remember his name or face, but I can still remember how I felt in his presence. He was also our babysitter when the adults went out to the lounges.

Wait! I remember his name: **Tennessee** was his name.

He was around 16 or 17 years old. And I remember him being very tall and muscular.

He would always come after May-May with a belt for no reason. And he'd always try to separate us, but I wouldn't let him...one night he did separate us though.

One night, I didn't feel May-May next to me as she always was. I immediately woke up and ran to look for her: she was in the kitchen sitting on Tennessee's lap! May-May

had to be around 2 or 3 years old at this time.

I felt a raging fire come over me because I felt that I knew his intentions...I don't know how or why I knew, but I knew his intentions were not good. And I was not going to let him hurt my sister.

I said, "May-May, get down off his lap!"

But, as I reached to grab her, he shoved me into the sharp corner of the wall. Immediately my face started bleeding, leaving a scar in the corner of my eye; I still have the scar to this day.

I jumped up quickly, grabbed May-May, ran back into the room, and balled up in a corner of the bed because I was so afraid of him coming into the room to get us.

But I prayed, "Jesus! Jesus! Jesus!" in my head. And he didn't come after us.

RISE ABOVE THE ORDINARY: The Life Behind Her Smile

CHAPTER 2

You're the one you've been waiting for... your resolve's been riding with you all along.

LPH

READY FOR SCHOOL

Ready For School

I remember it was warm outside, so it must be spring or summer; I'm not sure which.

My grandmother Burneda sent for me, but I didn't want to leave without my May-May. So, May-May came with me.

As always, I was happy to see my granny and aunts Yolanda and Nikki, my uncle Cortez (who was only 2 years older than me), and my friends that I play with when I come around.

My grandmother gave May-May and me a bath as soon as we walked through the door. And she had that look on her face as before when I told her I wasn't in school.

I remember her looking at the rag she used to wash us with and looking at the amount of dirt that came from it when she would rinse the soap out of the rag.

This time, we stayed with my grandmother for a long time because my mother had moved from Lisa's house to my Grandma Mae's house (mom's mother). I was happy about my mother moving too!

When it was time to go back home with my mom, my grandmother decided to keep me with her.

"You need to be in school." she said.

I was happy but saddened at the same time: I didn't want to be separated from my siblings.

I told my grandmother, "I need to go home because there is no one at home to take care of May-May and them."

She asked, "What are you talking about?!"

"Nothing." I said. I didn't tell her because I didn't want her to get angry like before.

But I prayed to God every day and night asking Him to protect my sisters and brothers.

The Best Year

While staying with my grandmother Burneda, I learned

how to assist her in cooking some of her favorite Sunday dinners.

I loved learning how to cook mustard and turnip greens with ham hocks, baked mac and cheese, sweet potatoes (which was my favorite) homemade cornbread, fried chicken, and peach cobbler for dessert!

Oh, how I loved to make her delicious chicken and dumplings...Ummm Ummm *Goodness*! Cooking soon became my stress reliever....I would cook *a lot*!

Those were the *best* times when I spent time with my grandma Burneda. But I just didn't like getting up early in the morning to do it.

The Summer of 1986 was the best year of my entire childhood... and even of right now today, as I think back on the Sunny, warm days of life in the Dearborn Home Projects on 29th and State Street!

My Grandma Burneda lived in the 2731 building.

I remember kids swinging on the swings as I would go up and down on the seesaw with my friends.

I remember guys playing basketball and the *Juicy Fruit* song blasting out of an apartment window.

I remember the older girls wearing *fresh* Jordache Jeans, K-Swiss shoes, and big dumb earrings, and sitting on the bench swaying and rocking to the beat.

I remember the project hallways smelling like Pine Sol Cleaner and Mop "N Glow Floor Shine as everyone deep cleaned their apartments on Saturdays.

Next thing you know, streetlights came on and all us kids went running in every direction to get home before our parents started screaming our names out the Window and saying like mine did "KISHA!!!!! Time to come in!"

I remember, at night we took our baths, went to bed, and fell asleep to the Voices of the older kids and adults still hanging out in front of the building.

Our apartment door stayed open throughout the night to catch that cool breeze that flowed through at night with nothing but a half screen placed between the doors to keep the mice out.

Then, the next day we were happy to see everyone all over again!

Life was so pure, innocent, safe, and loving throughout.

In September 1986 after the summer, my grandmother put me in school. But the school didn't know where to start with me because of my age; and my school records showed that I had attended school for only three months.

LAKISHA P HUNTER

The school told my grandmother, "We'll have to give her a test to see what she knows because she has only had three months of schooling."

The next day, I was given a test at the school; but the school was not expecting me to know anything at all.

The teacher asked me to count to 10, and I did. She asked me to name the colors she pointed to, and I did. She asked me to name the animals that she pointed to, and I did.

Then, she asked me, "Do you know your name and birthday?"

I told her "Yes," and I told her the answers to both.

She asked, "Do you know how to spell your name?"

I said, "Yes."

She put a piece of chalk in my hand, led me to the chalkboard, and I wrote and sounded out my full name just like my Daddy had taught me: "LAKISHA...PETRICE...HUNTER."

The teacher's mouth was left wide open in amazement and disbelief.

I continued writing more words on the board: *cat, rat, hat, hog, dog, red, Ted, glue, blue, honey, money, mom, dad, floor, door, sister, brother, car,* and *astronaut.*

The teacher was so astonished until she immediately called my grandmother and told her what had taken place.

My grandmother asked me, "Who taught you how to spell your name?"

"My Daddy." I said.

My grandmother then asked, "Well, how do you know those other things?"

I said, "I listened to Michael and my cousins do their homework and listened to them practice spelling words for their spelling tests like my Daddy told me to do."

That day, I was put in the 1st grade!

Great To Be Home

I spent the entire year of 1986 with my grandmother. But I was ready to go home because I missed my sisters and brothers.

My mom *promised* my grandmother I would continue to go to school when I moved back…but that never happened.

Instead, I was home now taking care of my *five* sisters and one brother.

Nothing had changed. My mom still didn't come home for days at a time. And, when she did come home, my stepfather would beat her until he was tired. But they were both heavy on drugs.

I remember my stepfather even breaking my mom's arm once.

We always lived from house to house. We hardly ever had food in the house because no one worked. And whatever monies my mom received from the government went to the loan sharks she borrowed from throughout the month.

I remember praying to God for deliverance out of this *hellhole*. (Yes, I used *those exact words*.)

Who taught or told me to pray? No one. It came instantly and easily at given moments.

Now, *I* had a way out, but my sisters and brother didn't; and I couldn't leave them like that.

We were used to sitting in the dark without light because my mom didn't pay the light bill. It was fun, tho! We would light candles, my cousins and I, and we would tell ghost stories.

My cousin Tiffany would act like she was Whitney Houston with a hairbrush in her hand singing *The Greatest Love Of All*.

We made the best out of hard times. I mean, what else could we do?

Again, I had a way out, but not without my sisters and brother.

Now, we had to move with my grandfather Dee-Dee. The move was ok…my grandfather Dee Dee, who was a lot of fun! It was ok because I really loved him.

May-May was a crybaby because she always wanted to be under my mom.

One day, my mom snuck out of the house, as she did often so that May-May wouldn't cry when she left. But when May-May saw that my mom was nowhere in the apartment, she started crying.

My grandfather thought, "I'll fix her!"

So, he took May-May into the hallway, left her by herself, and locked her outside on the porch.

May-May screamed! And I was MAD.

Although I knew that I could get in trouble, I ran and opened the door to let her in. Then, I turned and looked at my grandfather with such hatred until he saw it in my eyes. And at that moment, the love I had for him left. And I never felt the same for my grandfather after that day.

Gone again as usual, my mom took May-May and the twins with her but left my brother and me with a neighbor because my grandfather had a funeral to attend. I remember this like it was yesterday.

I can't remember what the guy watching us looked like, but I remember his sister. She was so pretty and nice to us.

We were sent in the back room to watch TV while they cleaned the house. Their friends came over and they began drinking and smoking weed.

Soon after they were done drinking and smoking weed, I could hear everyone leaving, even the sister.

"Now you're here with me." the guys say. "And I have something for both of you."

He entered the room with a belt. He told Michael and I, "Take off all of your clothes."

Michael asked, "What did we do? We didn't do anything to get a whooping."

He then slapped Michael in his face and told us, "Do what I say."

So, we did.

He then began whipping Michael with the belt. After he whipped Michael, he whipped me.

We had no clothes on…he whipped just our bare skin. And when he was done, he left the room.

Michael pulled me closer to him to comfort me. I was shaking.

Michael told me, "Hush. I will take care of you."

The guy came back into the room. But this time he was naked. His penis was huge.

He closed the door and told me, "Get on the bed."

Michael told him, "No."

He pushed Michael out of the way and threw me on the bed.

He told me to sit up, and I did. He then grabbed my head and told me, "Suck dick."

I said, "No."

He tried pulling my head towards his penis, but I wouldn't open my mouth. I then started to cry.

He said, "I see you are a feisty little number." I then grabbed the belt ran under the bed.

He then told Michael, "Call her from under the bed or I'm gone whip you again.

Since I didn't want Michael to get a whipping, I came out from under the bed on my own.

He then handed Michael the belt and told him, "Whip her."

Michael hit me with the belt.

He told him, "Hit her harder!"

But, while he was yelling at Michael, someone knocked on the door. He told us, "You better not make a sound!" We were afraid so we didn't.

He stepped out of the room to answer the door.

Michael told me, "Be brave. I'm not gone hurt you. I'm not gone hit you hard, but I want you to *scream* like I'm hitting you hard."

When the guy came back in the room, he was still naked and continued yelling at Michael, "Hit her with the belt!"

As Michael hit me with the belt, I remembered what he told me, and I screamed as if he was hitting me hard. This made the guy happy.

So, he instructed me to suck his penis again and this time I did open my mouth. He then grabbed my head and pushed his penis in my mouth.

Michael yelled, "NO!" and pushed the guy away from me.

As the guy rushed back towards me, Michael yelled, "I'll do it!"

The guy stopped. He said, "Ok."

He then took me into another bedroom which was next to where Micheal was. He locked me in the room by myself.

I remember getting angrier and angrier by the second.

In my anger, something was telling me to close my eyes and pray silently, so I did.

When all was over, he told us, "Don't to tell nobody because no one will believe you. And, if you do tell, I'll kill your mother."

So, we never told a soul.

CHAPTER 3

Don't accept and change to the point where your core and true self become unrecognizable... even unto *yourself*.

LPH

SCHOOL OF HARD KNOCKS

School Of Hard Knocks

I remember Don was the name of the "big shot" loan shark and drug man that my mom and stepfather dealt with.

He was mean but gave special attention to my mother. And even as a kid I knew there was more going on than meets the eye with Don and my mom. And I also knew that my stepfather knew the same thing.

Every month my mom's public aide check went to Don. He would take her to pick up her check and drop her back off at home broke.

Something went wrong once with my mom and Don. So wrong until my mom and stepfather came home with really bad bruises from Don pistol-whipping my mom.

I felt that my stepfather couldn't do much about Don beating my mom *because* Don had a gun.

I remember hearing my stepfather say, "Man, if he hadn't had that GUN!"

I saw in his face his feelings and his pride were so hurt. And he was angry enough to go retaliate and possibly *kill* the man too!

"Why do we have to live like this?" I asked God often. "I hate my life!"

Hustling To Survive

Michael, my big bother was around more now. Since he's three years older than me, we all did what he told us. We cleaned when he told us and went to bed when he told us.

We never had enough food to last throughout the week. So, Michael would go to school in the morning, mainly so he could eat breakfast and lunch, and then hustle at the grocery store and gas station after school.

He would help carry people's groceries or pump their gas for change.

Then, with whatever money he made, he would buy some pampers, bologna, corn king hot dogs, bread and sugar.

Michael would bring the food home and tell me to feed the kids and put them to sleep. We would eat sandwiches, sugar/bread and sugar water until we were full.

This was a regular thing for us. I knew my place and Michael knew his: He went to school and worked, and I took care of the kids.

One day after school, Michael came home empty handed because he didn't make any money. So, the kids were crying because they were hungry.

I remember Michael looking around for a minute, then leaving back out the door. I started to cry because I didn't know what to do.

A while later Michael came back. He still had no money; but he had a bag with 7 neck bones that the grocer gave him. Michael gave me the bag and told me, "Cook these and feed the kids."

I looked at him like he was crazy, and said, "I don't know how to cook! How am I supposed to cook these neck bones?!" I yelled.

Michael didn't respond to me. He laid down on the pallet of dirty clothes that we slept on for beds, put his hand behind his head and closed his eyes.

I was *so* mad. I sat at the kitchen table and started to cry, "God, help me! My life is a mistake! I was sent here by accident. I don't belong here. Please, please, PLEASE come and get me!"

Since the kids were asleep at this point, I went to sleep on the pallet next to them.

The kids went to bed without eating and they were hungry when they woke up.

My mom was asleep but didn't get up to attend to her hungry, wet, and crying kids.

So, I looked in the fridge and saw those same 7 neck bones that Michael brought in last night.

I sighed as I pulled the neck bones out of the fridge. I put them in a pot of water, put the pot on the stove, and turned on the fire. I waited 'til they turned brown as they did when I saw my grandmother cook neck bones before.

I remembered hiding a half bag of rice in a cabinet in the kitchen. I noticed that mice had chewed through the bag causing some to spill out. But the kids were hungry.

I cried.

I needed this rice, so I cooked it. Not knowing how to cook rice either, I put the rice in the pot with the neck bones until the water boiled out. I did not know to wash the rice or the neck bones prior to cooking them though.

We ate and everyone was content and full.

But, when my mother finally got up and saw what I had done, she fussed at me, "You could have burned the house down! Are you crazy?! Get your black, baldhead, fast pass out of my face!"

But I don't ever remember my mother talking to me in this way before. Something was very different about her.

My mom used to be so beautiful, with long curly hair down her back, and a body shaped like a 16-oz Coca-Cola bottle. But now she was not the same person.

I started to cry and so did the kids.

After that day, my whole attitude changed. I became angry, bitter, and ugly, even to myself.

I began walking around with my head down. I stopped smiling, and I don't remember smiling again in public for a very long time. I thought I was ugly.

I now believed what the kids in the neighborhood called me: *Black, Ugly, Dirty, Nappy-head, Stupid.* That's why I didn't go out much at that point.

After a while, Michael decided to take me to hustle with him. This made me realize that the two of us could make more money than one of us.

The money we made always went on food for the house.

But any money left over, my mother would find and take.

I remember one day Michael had a roll of money hidden in his underwear. I had gotten mad at Michael about something and told my mother that Michael had extra money.

My mom then stripped Michael of his clothes and took all his money he made that night. She then whipped him for lying.

I felt so bad about causing Michael to get a whipping until I never told on him again. And after that Michael never took me out to hustle with him again. I was hurt but I knew it was my own fault.

So, I went out on my own. I would pump gas and carry groceries. The men whom I asked to help would always give me more than the women.

The men would tell me, "You shouldn't be out here. Here's something extra. Now get off these streets before you get someone who means you harm!"

I took the money, but I didn't leave.

LAKISHA P HUNTER

Home Sweet Home Again

We finally have our own apartment on 46th and Calumet Streets. It was exciting not to have to live with other people.

For once my aunt needs to live with us instead of the other way around. It was cool because I like my aunt.

Things seem to be going well. I was back in school and so was May-May. And I don't remember going hungry at this location. I think it was because my aunt was living with us. When she fed her kids, she fed us too.

I could tell that she was a very good person and had a really big heart. She loved us. She never played favorites between her children and us. She even treated me like I was her blood.

I went to visit my grandfather named I.G. (my father's father) sometimes. I loved my grandfather, and he would do anything for me. I would spend weekends with him and his wife. She was the sweetest person you would ever meet.

I loved my grandfather, but I did not want to live with my grandfather.

They were from down south so Southern hospitality oozed out of them.

Sometimes my great Aunt Juanita (also called T.T.) would come to visit my grandfather when she learned I was over for the weekend. She'd take me to JCPenney to buy me clothes.

I remember one summer my mom took me to my grandfather's house just to visit, but my grandfather wanted me to stay. He handed my mom some money and moments later my mom told me she would pick me up the next day.

The next day came but my mom never came to get me. I stared out the window, day after day, watching for my mother to come around the corner. But before you knew it, the summer was over.

I missed my sisters and brother. I missed my mom and I wanted to go home. So, I wouldn't eat, and I started acting out and not minding my grandma Elnora.

One day Grandma Elnora noticed that I was sleeping a lot. She woke me and asked, "Are you feeling ok?"

I said, "I want to go home with my brother and sisters."

I heard her tell my grandfather what I said, and she said to him, "You shouldn't keep her here if she doesn't want to stay."

My grandfather replied, "But I paid Rochelle the money to let us keep her."

Grandma Elnora said, "But she's making herself sick because she wants to go home."

So, later that day, my grandfather sat me on his lap and told me, "I love you so much! I want you to stay here with me. I'll put you in school and take care of you. And I'll buy you *anything* you want. Do you want that?"

I remember telling him, "I want to go home."

Now, I loved my grandfather, but I did not want to live with him. So, that night, my grandfather took me back to my mom.

Busting through the door with all the excitement I could muster up just to see May-May, I couldn't believe she had grown so much! She had no front teeth when I left, but now her teeth are all filled in.

I remember my mom reaching out to hug me, but I kept playing with May-May and acting like I didn't hear her beckoning me to come give her a hug.

I was so hurt that my own mom would sell me to my grandfather until I really didn't know *how* to respond.

Still Growing

Now, I am in the 4th grade. Since I had been out of school for so long, and because of my age, the school counselors didn't know what grade to put me in.

The last grade I completed was first grade when I was 8 years old; but I hadn't been in school since. And now I'm 11yrs old, but too old for 2nd and 3rd grade. So, 4th grade it is.

I was very shy and afraid to speak. I looked down when I spoke to people. And I didn't smile a lot. The boys at school used to pick on me every day. They called me dirty, baldhead, black and ugly. The sad thing is I didn't say anything back because I believed what they were saying was true.

One day Corey Washington picked on me until I couldn't take anymore. So, I yelled, "Leave me alone! I am not bothering you!"

But he kept on and I blacked out.

The next thing you know, I was fighting! I just kept swinging and hitting without stopping. We were all over the place. The teacher broke us up, took us both into the washroom, and spanked us with a paddle.

I walked home from school by myself that day. I was so angry.

"I do not belong here! I wish I was dead. No one will miss me." I thought to myself.

So, as I walked home, I would think of different ways to kill myself. I really wanted to die, and I believed I could kill myself.

I'd think in my head, "God don't love me because, if He did, I would be dead by now!

(Now, why didn't I think that He would have delivered me by now instead of wanting to die? I'll expound on this later). He would have made me lighter in the skin. He would have given me the long and curly textured hair that the rest of my family has. He would have made me pretty."

Not beautiful, but pretty? Why didn't I care about beautiful but accepted pretty instead? Pray and ask God for revelation.to be continued…

CHAPTER 4

If *constant* compromise is the only way you can keep a person from leaving... slowly but *surely* you'll see one of the most important components of the relationship deteriorate... that component is YOU.

LPH

# HARD KNOCKS GET HARDER

Hard Knocks Get Harder

I remember that I turned the corner onto the block I lived on, and I saw a lot of people in front of the house we lived in. In the street in front of the house was a police car and a police paddy wagon.

So, I ran to the house to see what was going on. Once I made it to the house, I found out we were being set out and all our belongings were on the sidewalk.

My mother was sad.

I hung my head and asked God, "What's next?!"

I was always told that I was mature for my age, and I knew more than a child my age should. I was always thinking ahead.

I looked at my mom and said, "Well Mom, grandmother said I could live with her if I want. I'm sure she wouldn't mind it if May-May and I live with her for the summer. And Michael could live with granddaddy. You and the others can stay at your mother's house. This way, we wouldn't be over crowding anyone."

My mother just started crying.

I went to live with my grandmother, and my mom and my other siblings did too. I was so happy that we were all together.

Parent Training

I remember my grandmother coaching my mother on how to take care of her children, how to shop for food, and how to cook. My mother seemed to be attentive.

I'm not sure how much later, but we finally moved out of my grandmother's house and moved in with my aunt and her kids... again.

Soon after moving in with my grandmother, two women from my former school came to the house to see why I haven't been attending school (Truant officers).

The two women were persistent. They came by daily to investigate why I was not in school. I'm not sure what excuse my mother gave the two women, but their persistence must have scared my mother because I was in school the next day.

I'm not sure how my grandmother found out, but she did. I was at her house one weekend, and she asked me about the truant officers who came to the house.

I told my grandmother, "I'm back in school now and everything is fine."

My grandmother sighed. She looked at me and said, "Little girl. That's what you are, a little girl; not a grown woman." And then she walked away.

I was puzzled for a minute.

Moments later, she came back with a sheet of paper and a pencil. She wrote on the first line her name, address, and telephone number. She said, "Memorize everything on this paper. If anyone comes to try to take you away, call me."

Needless to say, I learned everything she wrote on that sheet of paper before the weekend was over.

I still missed a lot of days out of school because I wasn't awakened on time or when I woke up no one was home but me and the kids who I would never leave home alone.

RISE ABOVE THE ORDINARY: The Life Behind Her Smile

May-May was at home a lot also. And Stephanie and Steve are growing up.

Stephanie was funny as a child. She laughed at anything and sometimes for no reason at all.

I remember Stephanie being tender headed with hair down to her behind. Her hair was so thick and curly, and so tangled that I would have to use water to brush it out so it wouldn't hurt. She still cried though.

Steven was quiet but silly too. He would laugh because Stephanie laughed. But Steven was a different child. He rocked back and forth on the couch all the time. Every day was the same thing: he would just rock for hours on the couch.

Danielle (Nikki) also had very long, thick and curly hair. Nikki was a girly girl. She acted like a grown woman from the time she came out the womb, very jazzy at the mouth and inquisitive.

She knew who did and said what. Whatever you wanted to know Nikki knew it and would tell you if you asked, but she didn't volunteer information.

Then, we have Donnell (Boona) who is the baby. He was smart and picky. He watched everything everybody did. He didn't talk but he would watch everything and everybody.

I knew all my siblings like a book. Who hit who first, and who would lie or who would tell the truth. But the four of them had a special bond.

They always took up for each other. One didn't like for the other to get in trouble. Sometimes Nikki didn't care and would tell everything. Boy was she funny!

It's that time again…moving. This time into our own apartment on 43rd and Shields, down the street from my mother's mom. I didn't like that lady (my mother's mom) because she was mean. We had to go to bed before the streetlights came on. Every night we went to bed at the same time - 7pm, even in the summertime.

While the other kids were outside playing, we were in bed - streetlights weren't even on yet!

When she'd wake us in the morning, we ate breakfast. Her cooking was umm-umm good though…grandma-maa could *throw down* in the kitchen! Oh Yes, we *always* ate good.

Then, by 9:00 am, we were sent outside to play whether we wanted to go out or not. We couldn't come back into the house until it was time to come in except to use the washroom.

Grandma had 10 kids, and my mom was her 7th child. She was no joke. You moved when she said move and you talked when she said talk. If not, she would whip your butt *"'til the sun comes up"* is what she would tell us.

But I never gave her a reason to whip me that long. And if she did whip me that long, I would call and tell my other grandmother and *she* would handle her.

I thought my other grandmother could conquer the world. Everyone in the projects called her "Lieutenant Bennett" (her last name was Bennett). Grandma (my father's mother) didn't play – she was about 5-feet 7-inches, weighed about 280 pounds, and her bark was as tough as her bite - but she had a big heart.

Whenever she cooked, she would always prepare a lot because she knew that, once word got out that she had cooked, it seemed like friends from everywhere came running with their plates and bowls. And I loved it!

Forever In My Memory

I remember when I did get what I believe was my *first* whipping, but not from my mom. My mom didn't spank/whip us because we, for the most part, didn't do anything that gave a reason for us to be spanked.

As kids, even without having much, we had fun playing with our cousins and friends - Lakisha and Felicia - who lived down the street. There was an older sister and older brother, so 4 of them altogether.

Their parents were super cool and nice to everyone. Mrs. McClain, their mom, was a schoolteacher; and their father, Mr. McClain, was a policeman.

As you can see, Felicia and Kisha had the same first names as me and May-May. And we did *e-ve-ry-thing* together…even slept outside on their porch overnight with covers and sleeping bags!

Every day we'd play until we were called inside. There was no judgement in their eyes or heart about what we had or didn't have. If Felicia had snacks, she made sure May-May had snacks.

They would let us play with their toys, jump rope, play basketball, or whatever we wanted. It didn't matter what it was, we were true friends with a very tight bond: we were tighter than 10 toes in two socks!

One day we all were playing softball in Henderson School's parking lot over the summer: everyone from Sheilds was playing. When the ball was hit in my direction, I tried to catch the ball, but the ball hit the tip of my index finger and caused me to be in excruciating pain; so much pain until I yelled the "M-F" curse word.

I could not *believe* this word came out of my mouth! It *literally* just *slipped…out…*of my mouth!!

When we were done playing, my cousins told my Aunt Karen that I used the "MF" word. My aunt called me into the house and asked me, "Did you say the 'M-F' word as they say you did?"

I said, "I *did* say it, but the ball jammed my finger, and it just slipped out! But I *promise* I won't say it again!"

She said, "Ooh! So, it just *"slipped out"* huh?! Well, this *belt* about to slip on your ass! TAKE off my pants and lay across the couch!"

Then, she had my uncle and my cousin hold my arms and legs to make my body be stretched out.

She got this BIG, *thick*, leather belt with holes in it to whip me.

I could not move! I was faced downward with one cousin holding my arms and the other holding my legs and wearing nothing but my panties and a shirt.

My aunt beat me with this BIG…black…thick…*genuine leather* belt that had holes in it. Every hit hurt so bad until, when I opened my mouth to scream, nothing came out.

Every blow took my breath away. It was one of the most unforgettable days of my life!

When she was done whipping me, she sent me outside to play.

I remember I could not sit on my bottom *at all* that day. With hurt in her eyes, my friend Kisha didn't say a word.

She saw me come out of the house from across the street, she came over and consoled me while I stared afar off wishing in my head that I would die.

I snuck to the payphone to collect-call my grandma Burneda to tell her what happened.

The next day my grandma came and got me. She cussed out my mother and said, "If yo' ugly-ass sister *ever* whips my grandbaby like that again, I'll give her a beatin' *she* will never forget!"

New Day More Trouble

The Truant officers stopped coming to the house, but a new lady started coming to the house. This lady was from The Department of Children and Family Services (DCFS). I'm not sure who called DCFS, but the rep said they were told that my mother was on drugs and that her children were home often without adult supervision.

Needless to say, when the lady came to the house, no adults were home. I opened the door and she asked, "Is your mother home?"

I said, "No."

She asked, "Who is home with you?"

I said, "No one except my sister May-May. But we are on our way back down the street to my grandmother Mae's house." Of course, I was lying. Somehow, I knew that if I were to say anything different, there would be trouble.

The lady then asked, "Can I follow you down to your grandmother's house?

I said, "Yes."

Once we got to my grandmother Mae's house, the lady introduced herself to my grandmother, and my grandmother immediately got nervous.

The lady then said to my grandmother, "Don't worry. I just want to ask a couple of questions."

As the lady began asking the questions, it became apparent that my mother had been warned that the DCFS would be sending people to come to the house to check on things, but either my mother did not pay attention, or she didn't take them seriously.

The lady completed asking my grandmother some questions and then asked to speak to me since I was the oldest child in the house at the time.

My grandmother called me into the front room. I stood in front of the lady, and she told me, "Be truthful. What is your name and age."

Now, I can tell that this lady was very smart and that she would know if I was lying. So, I answered her questions truthfully.

She asked, "Are you in school?"

I said, "Yes."

She said, "Have you ever been left at home alone?"

I said, "Yes."

She asked, "Is there a refrigerator in this house."

I said, "Yes."

"Is there food in it?" she asked.

I said, "No."

She asked, "Do you have a stove at home?"

I said, "Yes."

"Is the gas on?"

I said, "No."

I can see in my grandmother's face that I was not answering the questions the way that she thought that I should have or the way she wanted me to. So, she would jump in between each question to teach me what I should have said so I would change my answers.

Then, the lady spoke in a rough tone to my grandmother saying, "Do not interfere with my investigation please!"

She continued with her investigation by asking other questions like if I had clean clothes, when was the last time I had a bath, etc.

In the mist of answering the social worker questions, I noticed that I wasn't helping by telling the truth, and that I may have made things worse. So, I started shaking and my eyes filled with tears. *"What* have I *done?"* I thought.

The lady noticed and stopped asking questions. Then she said to me, "You will be all right. You are very mature for your age."

Then, she looked at my grandmother and said, "Tell her mom I will be back on Tuesday." She gave my grandmother a paper and said, "These are the things that I will be looking for when I come back."

After the lady left, my grandmother looked at me like she could beat the *hell* out of me. She told me, "Go to the back room until your mother comes home!"

When my mother came home, my grandmother told her what happened, and she was upset. She was teary-eyed. She kept asking me, "Why would you say there was no food in the house?!"

My grandmother standing on the sideline 'co- signing' asking me, "Yeah, why would you tell that lady the truth?

Do you *want* to be taken away and put in a foster home where no-one could find you, and you would be separated from your sisters and brother?!"

CHAPTER 5

Don't accept and change to the point where your core and true self become unrecognizable... even unto *YOURSELF!*

LPH

THE RISE BEGINS

LAKISHA P HUNTER

THE RISE BEGINS

I remember that those words my grandmother said about my answers to the DCFS lady is all I could hear in my head until I was maybe 20 years old.

"I am usually quick on my toes! Why didn't I think of those things my grandmother said?! My God!! I *can't* be taken away from my mother or my siblings! I would die!! God, *please* help me! Please! I need you *so* bad! **Please**!!... Can you hear me? I hate myself! I hate myself!...It hurt so badly!"

I was screaming these words inside my head as tears begin to fall from my face onto the windowpane that I was looking out of, while looking up towards God.

WHEW!

The lady from DCFS came back like she said she would. And we passed the home inspection.

See, what had happened was…..after the lady left warning that she would return, my father's mother and some more family members came to the house to get things in order before the lady returned for her inspection visit.

Now, since the lady forgot to bring the lead tester, she didn't know that the paint chips on the floor and walls had lead in them.

After the visit, I was relieved that no one had to be taken away. But the lady *did* tell my mom that she will be back; but this time it will be unannounced. She also informed my mother that a different lady named Pat Simmons will be calling to help us stay on track.

Well, true enough, Pat Simmons (our caseworker) came by some days later. She was so nice. And after a few visits, I could see that Pat really did care about my mother and our family's well-being:

Pat would notice some things that were wrong but give my mother chance after chance to get the wrong things right. She forewarned my mother of when her supervisor would be coming to our house and what she would look for during her visit, etc.

So, you can see why I was certain that Pat really cared.

In 1988, my aunt Betty and her kids (my cousins) moved to Indiana. We went to visit, and we had a blast; so much until I wanted to stay longer. Since school was about to start again,

I couldn't stay longer. But Pat warned my mother that it would not be good if I didn't start going to school on a regular basis.

Well, we were doing well for a while. I was going to school and my mom was home more. The drugs and alcohol still existed; and so did the beatings that my stepfather would give my mother whenever he got too high or drunk.

One night, my stepfather was beating my mom so bad that Michael couldn't take it anymore.

Michael jumped in the fight trying to help defend my mother. My stepfather was very strong, and he tossed Michael completely across the room with one arm; then, Michael got hurt.

But we all were screaming at my stepfather, "Leave my mother alone!!"

We really loved our mother. She was a lot of fun and she spoiled everyone when she was around.

She was so beautiful to me!

Here We Go Again

I'm not sure what happened to cause this, but things were starting to fall off again. I wasn't going to school and food was short.

Pat told my mother, "The truant officers are back on your case about Lakisha not attending school, Rochelle!"

My mother had plans to go back to Indiana to visit my aunt. But

Pat told my mother, "Don't go back to Indiana either. I'm serious!" But my mom didn't listen.

The next morning, there was a knock on the door. May-May and I were asleep, and no adults were at home.

Our ceiling fell in due to the toilet leaking from the bathroom upstairs directly over our apartment. There was poop leaking in too every time the people upstairs flushed the toilet.

My stepdad did his best to stay on top of cleaning it up so that none of the kids would touch it. Day after day he would clean up this poop because he truly cared about us. You could really see his heart when he wasn't drinking.

Yes, he did beat my mom when she didn't come home for days at a time and when he was under the influence of drugs and alcohol, be he did more for us than most.

How can I appreciate a person like my stepfather? He was sometimes bending his back and on his and knees scrubbing dirty clothes in the tub for hours on end to make sure we had clean clothes to go outside and play in. He did his best to comb the kid's hair so it wouldn't be all over their heads.

And Yes, sometimes he would clean. But I loathed him on the other hand for what he had done to my mom.

My stepdad contracted tuberculosis because of cleaning up the poop. We lived under these conditions for weeks. Our house started to smell like an outhouse. Dirty clothes were everywhere, and my mother and four younger siblings were gone to Indiana.

The knocks on the door got louder so I answered the door.

The lady at the door asked, "Why aren't you at school?! And where is your mother?!"

"My mother is asleep, and I have a cold." I quickly responded.

She said, "Ok." And then she walked away.

A few minutes later, there was *another* knock on the door. But this time a different lady was at the door - the social worker. She came to take us away.

May-May started crying *hysterically* as the lady picked her up off the couch and told her to come and go with her. She walked us down the street to my grandma Mae's house to tell what was going on, and to see if she could keep us from going to a foster home.

While her emotions were all over the place, my grandma said, "I can't take them."

My Auntie Lillian, who was around 18 years old at the time, asked, Can I watch them?"

The lady said, "No." Then, she said to my sister and me, "Come on and let's go."

My Auntie Lillian then said aggressively, "Can I at *least* comb my niece's (May-May) hair?!"

The Lady paused and said, "Yes." Then, Auntie Lillian combed May-May's hair.

I'm not sure where we were taken initially. But Pat came there and got May-May and me. Michael was still in school.

Pat took us to a place called Cook County Courts for The Department of Children and Family Services.... or something like that.

I remember Pat walking back and forth with her hand on her head and fear in her eyes.

"Why didn't my mom listen to Pat? What was she thinking? She told her that, if she left town, we would be taken away! Did she *want* the state to take us away? Did she not want us?" were my thoughts racing through my head.

The more I thought about what my mom just put us through, the angrier I became.

May-May's crying was getting on my nerves. Whatever patience I *had* was shot.

I think we had been sitting in the same spot for about 5 *hours* now. And Pat was on the phone a lot, making phone calls the whole time - whoever for whatever.

I could tell the offices were closing by how empty the halls were becoming.

Finally, Pat came over to check on us, and she looked exhausted.

I asked her, "When are we leaving to go home?"

She said, "You can't go back home. I've been on the phone all day trying to find someone to take you...all seven of you."

I told her, "Call my grandmother."

She said, "I already tried asking your grandma Mae, and she said No."

I jumped up and said, "Not her! My *other* grandmother."

Pat asked, "Who?"

I said, "Burneda Bennett!"

Pat asked, "Do you know the number?"

I said, "Sure..." and told her the number. "My grandmother said that, if someone comes and tries to take me away, call her and she'll come and get me."

Pat looked at me with relief for about ten seconds. Then she looked at me like she could kill me. She said, "Well baby, why didn't you tell me this before now".

And I said, "Because you didn't ask me." (when really I didn't tell her because my grandmother said she would only take me, and I didn't want to be taken away from my sister May-May)

Needless to say, Pat went ahead and took May-May and I to my grandmother; and she took Michael later.

Reality Bites Us All

After my mother learned of what happened, she took the train back to Chicago the next day. When she entered the Cook County Courts, my other siblings were taken from my mom as well.

Pat had already talked to my grandmother about taking the other four, so they came to live with us as well.

YAY! All seven of us are together again! I could have burst with joy when I saw Steven, Stephanie, Nikki, and Boona come through the door!

I looked them over very closely to make sure they were ok too.

Now, I'm drilling them: Are you scared? What did momma say? What did my stepfather say?

Nikki said, "Momma was crying while we were on the train."

Learning that my mom was crying made me feel a little better because it meant that she cared for her children. But then I felt sad because I also realized my mom is miserable.

I remember not seeing my mother for a while because she wasn't allowed to come to the house. I'm not sure if she called, but I'm almost certain that she didn't.

But we were not a problem to my grandmother - I made sure of it!

We would clean the room before she would ask. And when we played, we were careful not to make a lot of noise that would irritate her or make her upset.

My grandmother never complained about having to care for her three kids who still lived at home, plus me and six other children who are not related to her. She treated all of us like we all were her own.

Since all eleven of us living in a three-bedroom project apartment was beyond crowded, my grandmother felt the need to look for a house. So, she began looking.

Yolanda helped my grandmother out a lot with taking care of us. She made sure we bathed and ate, and she made sure May-May, Michael, and I went to school.

I remember that, while Yolanda was working at Wendy's, she knew that there was a good chance that my mother wouldn't have anything for us for Christmas.

So, for two Christmases in a row, Yolanda brought me gifts. And, not just me, but she brought gifts for all of my siblings too!

Sometime later, Yolanda became pregnant and moved out with her child's father. She told my grandmother everything and my grandmother was happy; but she was sad at the same time because this meant that Yolanda wouldn't be able to help her take care of all of us.

This also meant that finding a house or apartment big enough wasn't a problem any longer since my grandmother couldn't raise all of us on her own.

No one told me this, but this is something that I just knew.

So, I prayed and asked God, "What should I do? How do I handle this? We are going to be split up, and my siblings are going to be lost in the system and I will never see them again. God, *please* tell me what to do. *Please* keep my siblings together wherever they go!"

I sobbed and begged God all night on what to do.

I'm not sure about how long after this - maybe a month - Pat came to take my sisters and brothers away. My Grandmother had explained what was going to happen a couple of days prior to her coming.

On that morning, I got up early. I remember my body being in so much pain until I told my grandmother. My grandmother thought I was saying I was pain just to stay home from school. But that was not the case.

As I was preparing for school, l told everyone to sit up on the couch. Then, I reiterated what my grandmother had said to us the previous day.

I told them, "Stick together. When *one* fight, all fight." I looked at them and whispered so that none but them could hear what I was saying. "I love y'all. And, when I get big enough, I am going to come and find all of y'all and you gonna live with me."

Stephanie asked, "You promise?"

I said, "I Promise!"

We hugged and I went to school. This was the saddest day of my life!

CHAPTER 6

Be diligent in your actions and satisfied in all your givings. Saying this to say *Have No Regrets*.

#YouCan'tUnscrambleScrambledEggs.

LPH

THE RISE MAKES CHANGES

THE RISE MAKES CHANGES

I remember months later that my grandmother found an apartment in the Englewood area on 55th and Carpenter.

From this point forward my life would forever be changed.

Prior to moving here, I was told that this area was nothing nice. You must know how to fight in order to survive or go to school in this area. But I didn't care about any of this; all I cared about was my younger siblings.

During this summer, I had 4 fights within 1 month. This is the reason I decided to join a gang. I had to protect my sister, and being a part of a gang was the only way I knew to do that.

John Hope Community Academy is the name of the school I attended. And my grandmother didn't play about school: Come rain or high water, blizzard or maybe a tornado, sick or on your death-bed, every school-aged child had to go to school.

But by this time, I'm at the point of hating school.

For one, I was stupid: I'm put in my right (grade 6th), and I can read and spell on a 6th grade level, but lacked the comprehension of a 6th grader.

My schooling timeline went like this:

GRADE	ATTENDANCE
Headstart	None
Kindergarten	None
First Grade	Yes
Second Grade	No
Third Grade	No
Fourth Grade	1 month
Fifth Grade	½ school year

Since the school officials knew my schooling history, what the *hell* did they expect me to do in 6th grade!

Second, I'm the darkest-skinned person in my class, which was enough to get roasted on a daily basis. My clothes weren't name-brand like 98% of my class and I'm stupid!

Could This Be Love?

On October 19, 1989, as I was switching class, I noticed this dark, super-cute boy who was in 8th grade. I was so fascinated with him. He was very popular and a well-known member of the gang I was in.

He was a leader of the school we attended [John Hope]. And he always had an entourage with him.

Every now and then, he would catch me looking at him, but I never spoke to him – I would just look away.

He was my first *real* crush. His name was Damone.

One day I decided to cut school with my home girl and fellow gang member, Char.

This was my first time cutting class at school. But a week prior, Mrs. Robinson, our homeroom teacher, saw that I was hanging out with Char, and she pulled me aside one day.

She told me, "Be careful hanging with Char., She's more mature than you and she is bad news." Although I *heard* her, I didn't <u>listen</u> to her.

When we cut school, I followed Char to a nearby building where all the bad boys hung out. We called these places

"The Tilt" - an apartment with no supervision; just kids who cut school, were gang affiliated, and had guns and drugs were hidden in these places.

As we went into the building, I was terrified because no one knew me at the time because I wasn't popular. I didn't know if I was going to be clowned by everyone or what. I just didn't know what to expect.

We knocked on the door, and one of the guys answered. There were only 3 people in there at the time. Char introduced me to them and told me, "I'll be right back." as she walked to the back room with 2 of the guys.

I was left in the front room with the other guy. He said, "Come check out something in this other room."

I followed him to the other room to see what he had to show me. (Talk about naïve!)

Once we got in the room, he closed the door behind us and started unfastening his pants.

I asked him, "What are you doing?"

He said "*You* know what it is. Drop those drawz!"

I said "NO! I'm not doing anything with you!"

He said "Yes you are! My guys back there running a train on ya' girl and I'm about to hit that!" Then, he grabbed my arm.

I yelled, "STOP!" and pushed him away from me.

As he was charging back at me, he yelled "I'm gonna take that shit."

Suddenly, someone knocked on the outside door. He left out of the room and went to the door to see who was knocking on the door with his gun in his hand.

Whoever was at the door, the guy let him in. I heard their conversation.

The guy who just entered the apartment asked, "Who y'all got up here?"

The guy said, "Char and one of her lil' female friends who think she isn't givin' it up, but I'm gonna fu&$ her ass!"

The guy who just came in said "Oh yeah?! Let me see who this chicken-head is."

The door to the room where I was opened, and who but Damone opened the door!

Damone looked at me and then looked at the other guy and said, "*This* the girl you said was trying to play hard to get and you gonna take it?!"

The guy said "Yeah."

Damone took the guy's gun out his hand, threw the gun on the bed, and beat the boy up very badly.

The other guys ran into the room to see what was going on and broke them up.

Damone told him, "If you *ever* try anything like that with her again, you *will* get violated! She's not a chicken head! She's my girlfriend!

Then Damone grabbed my hand and escorted me out of the building, leaving Char inside.

He walked me to Lowe Street, which was 1 block away from the building, and said, "Go home and never hang out with Char again. She's a hood rat!"

As I was starting to walk away, I turned and asked him, "Wait! Am I your girlfriend?'

He yelled back at me, "HELL Naw! Now get your ass back to school!"

But later in that school year, I was his girlfriend.

Mrs. Robinson was right about Char: being with her almost got me raped.

This is not what our gang is about. Damone reported that guy anyway and he was dealt with by the leaders in our region.

Mrs. Robinson was an angel in the form of a teacher who always looked out for me. Although I was a challenge to her as a student, she never stopped trying to push me to make better decisions.

Sometimes her husband would come to the school to visit and sometimes surprise her. I could tell that she mentioned me to him because he made it his business to ask me how I was doing and to also joke around with me. Mr. Robinson was hilarious.

Mrs. Robinson even allowed me to write letters to her husband, Frank Robinson, who also worked with at-risk students. Mrs. Robinson saw that I was carrying a lot of anger and thought I could use writing to talk about what had me in such a strong dominating disposition.

I must say it was a relief to get out some of the things going on in my head.

Sometimes Mr. Robinson would write back to me and encourage me to keep writing and staying focused by letting Mrs. Robinson know when I needed help in understanding assignments.

Mrs. Robinson was also a very *classy* lady from the south. She was very smart. And, although she had proper speech, you could hear that southern drawl come out at times.

RISE ABOVE THE ORDINARY: *The Life Behind Her Smile*

Kisha and Damone. We were best of friends. Everyone knew who he was, and now everyone knew who *I* was.

We were Bunny and Clyde. He *stayed* in fights and got arrested often, as did I. And, I soon became one of the leaders in my school.

Separated Sisters For Now

I didn't play around but I also had a soft spot for those who weren't as popular and those who were dark-skinned, considered ugly and, unpopular.

Some I could save from getting jumped on, and others I couldn't.

There was this one girl everyone called "monkey" girl, Tasha. She was picked on every day after school. She dressed nicely, but she was really dark and not too attractive.

One day I heard that she was going to get jumped after school. So, I put out the word that, if anyone would have bothered her, they would have to answer to me!

Then, I sent a message to Tasha, "Tell anyone who bothers her that you're my cousin. And no one will mess with you again." And no one bothered her anymore.

Soon, Tasha and a few more of her friends approached the neighborhood candy store. They said to me, "We want to pay for your candy." And another one of them said, "I want to be just like you, join the gang and your posse, and follow you!"

I looked at her and my heart was saddened. At the time, I didn't know why, but sadness came over me. So, I walked out of the store without my candy and went home.

Since my uncle and I hung out so much and did pretty much everything together, I was considered a" tomboy." I played sports, climbed trees, dressed in baggy clothes, and I was a gangbanger.

The end of the school year is approaching, and my grades were horrible. So horrible that I was not promoted to the next grade level.

I sat in class and did minimum work. Instead of telling the teacher I didn't know how to do the work, I sat and wrote poems and drawing gang signs all over my paper.

This school year I spent most of the school year suspended and in lockup. I was arrested over 10 times for mob action, and assault and battery. I also got in so much trouble with my teachers that I received 26 parent conferences where my grandmother had to come to the school. And I was suspended for fighting 4 times at 10 days each time.

The next school year I had to repeat the 6th grade. I was so embarrassed.

All of my friends/gang members were in a high grade level, and I felt really stupid. I knew I was at *least* smarter than *this*. So, I wanted to try to do better this year.

As classes began, I found myself in the same class as the girl Mattie that I fought in front of the corner store when I first moved to 55th and Carpenter.

I saw that she was fearful of me, so I didn't say anything to her.

The teacher I had this year was Mrs. Catherine Walker. She was a cool teacher that cared a lot about her students. She was tough though.

Mrs. Jackson was another good teacher who meant business. She was strict. She was my World Social Studies teacher. She was known for spoiling her homeroom class because they really were a smart class.

Mrs. Jackson was hilarious too! And she knew all the tricks we pulled as students; we couldn't get anything past her because she was too swift on her toes.

Most of my new friends were in her class. This year my friends changed. I was still doing me outside of school, but not so much while in school.

In this school year I was determined to do better. I was determined not to make people feel like they had to act as if they were my mother to show love to me.

Back on the home-front, my sister Falisha and I were drifting apart.

I remember telling her that she couldn't hang with me anymore because, whenever she would get mad at me, she would tell my grandmother some of the things I would do in the streets, influencing my grandmother to put me on punishment.

I can still remember the day I told her she could no longer hang out with me.

Now, about 30 years later, I understand that I abandoned my sister to some extent. And now I can understand why our relationship as teenagers, and now as adults, is the way it is: I feel she's angry at me for abandoning her.

She's night, and I'm day. We argue. And we fight.

Falisha started making her own friends, which was great. But I still kept an eye on her. And people in the area knew she was my sister, and she was not to be touched.

New Life New Standards

As for the crew that I hung around with outside of school, Double Nickel Posse is what we called ourselves. We hung out every day, still fighting of course. We banged hard, took no prisoners, and walked and talked rough and tough.

Knowing that I had people to look out for me, and I for them, felt good.

Although we hung out and really looked out for each other, I was still different from them. They were very well dressed, wore designer clothes, and had more freedom than I did. The boys were so interested in them.

Damone was my boyfriend, but I only kicked it with him around the school and around the house. I didn't want to be around him and the other side of gang-affiliated life he lived.

I knew it was way more dangerous than what I was doing at the moment, so he kept me from it.

Damone and I were like Bunny and Clyde. There was never a time that I couldn't rely on him to have my back, and he relied on me to do the same.

The closer we got the more I did for him. He stashed guns and drugs, and I eventually started prepping and bagging the drugs.

One day he decided to show me how to shoot a gun, a .357 magnum. I was standing on the back porch of "The Tilt."

He stood behind me as we pointed the gun out of the window at a tree in the next yard. He showed me how to breathe while holding the gun, and then while my finger was on the trigger.

Damone said, "At the count of three, pull!"

I pulled and fell backward. The recoil kickback was so strong that it blew me back almost to the wall. But my "Clyde" caught me.

One day, something changed in Damone, and he didn't want me around as much. He wouldn't allow me to hide guns anymore. He wouldn't let me sell or help with the drugs anymore.

We still hung out and sometimes cut school together, but it was a little different.

In later years, I asked Damone what that was about.

He said, "I felt guilty and knew what I had you doing was wrong and dangerous. I didn't want anything to happen to you."

He became my first sexual experience

CHAPTER 7

Settling for the possibility that you may be wrong to keep from a hurtful truth only prolongs the healing that will make the probability of the inevitable obtainable.
#Acceptit or #NOT

LPH

CHANGES BRING BETTER DAYS

CHANGES BRING BETTER DAYS

I remember that 1991-1992 was a very good year. My grandmother called me, May-May, and Michael in her room and told us that my mom had another baby, a girl, and named her Verlene after my stepfather's mother.

I was shocked that my mom had another baby. "What was she thinking?! How *dare* she have another baby!!" was my thoughts to myself.

Thank God that my mom's sister Stina allowed my mom and stepdad to live with her after she had Verlene!

My mom and Aunt Stina were like oil and water. Stina didn't drink or smoke, nor did she do drugs. To this day, Aunt Stina is the only one of Grandma Mae's 10 children who never did any of those things.

She loved watching soap operas and westerns and reading novels.

I don't remember seeing Aunt Stina a lot. But I do remember that, when I did see her, she was nice.

Mistakes And Good Times

A social worker was assigned to my sister Verlene after she was born because of my mom's history of drug abuse. And five years later, my mom was required to complete a drug test and failed the test.

Once my mom failed the drug test, she was summoned to court and instructed to bring my baby sister Verlene with her. My mom was unaware that DCFS was going to take Verlene from her.

The caseworker informed my aunt Stina what was going to take place at court. My aunt Stina asked the caseworker if Verlene could stay with her instead of being given to strangers. The caseworker informed the court of aunt Stina's request, and the court awarded my aunt Stina custody of my sister Verlene.

I thank God for my aunt Stina accepting my sister Verlene to live with her while she already had 4 of my mom's kids living at home with her.

Prior to this, I remember seeing my baby sister Verlene. My mom and stepdad brought her to my grandmother's birthday party on Christmas Eve. My grandmother and Yolanda knew Verlene was coming so they made sure Verlene had toys under the Christmas tree to take home with her.

Verlene looked just like Stephanie when Stephanie was her age. She had long, black, beautiful curly, wavy hair and pretty skin.

She looked a lot like my mother. We *loved* our baby sister!

Later when she was older, around 6 or 7, I would go get her and buy her whatever she wanted. Even when she was in middle school, I made sure she had everything we didn't when we were growing up.

During this year my dad came to the house to see me. He was looking good. My mom only came to the house once a year, which was Christmas Eve, on my father's mother's birthday.

Everyone came around when it was my grandmother's birthday to celebrate. She had the best parties!

During this time, every cousin, aunt, and other relatives would come "from under their little rocks" to have a good time with Grandma.

I always looked forward to the family gathering every year.

Since we had been separated from our siblings, my sister and I would go once a month to visit my other siblings at a community center organized by DCFS.

This visit was so hard to do! We had fun while visiting with each other, but it was so hard to depart from my siblings and leave them behind.

Every visit, my sister Stephanie would whisper in my ear "Remember you said you were coming to get us. You gonna get us, right?"

I always assured her that I would. But I had gotten so involved in what I was doing that I almost forgot about this promise.

When I would get home after visiting with my siblings, I would feel so guilty, thinking to myself, "Why am I here and they're not? How could this be fair?"

With tears streaming, I prayed:

"God please forgive me for forgetting and abandoning my brothers and sisters! I pray that you forgive me so

that they will forgive me. I pray to get them back when I get grown. But until then, keep them together. Don't let anyone separate them. Don't let anyone rape or beat them. And God, don't let them get lost in the system where I can't find them. In Jesus name, Amen."

Gang Life vs. Good Influencers

This year I'm in the 7th grade, and all of my original friends have graduated, even Damone.

I had many fights in this 7th grade year. I had so much I was dealing with mentally concerning my siblings, and fighting had become my regular/vice sometimes. Sometimes cooking with grandma wasn't able to subside the rage I was feeling.

Every couple of months when I would see my siblings at court, we'd stand before the judge and my response year after year remained the same…every time.

The judge asked me, "What do you need? Or what do you want me to grant you?"

"I want custody of my brothers and sisters," I said without flinching.

The judge would smirk and then she'd say, "You're too young to get custody of your brothers and sisters. But when you get old enough, you can get them."

After leaving court or after seeing them at the family connection center I'd be full of anger and guilt.

With all of these shootings going on and my original crew leaving, I had to maintain the rep I built for myself. So, I had to show myself tough; so much so until I became a bully - to the point where the bus stops within a 5-block radius weren't safe.

While walking around with my girls after school, whomever I would see standing at the bus stop, my crew and I would jump on them.

Innocent girls and guys from all over were in jeopardy of us jumping on them. If I didn't know you or have not seen you before, I would walk up and steal off you, sometimes just straight body slam you to the ground for no reason at all! And, then my crew would finish you off by stomping you like you stole something.

That's just the way it was.

Now, I remember this day like it was yesterday. My Damone asked me, "Do you want to be a first lady?"

I was thinking, "What do I ask him?"

"You know what I'm talking about?" he says. "I need somebody at the school to hold shit down on the girls side, and I can handle shit on the outside."

I knew everything there was to know about the gang I was in: My list was on lock and so was my crew. I could split lit (gang literature/language) at any given moment. I agreed to be the first lady. So, he took me to our leadership, and they explained to me my assignment and who I was to report to. And here you have a gang leader.

This was another pivotal moment for me as it relates to how I looked at myself, and how others looked at me.

Mrs. Johnson was my 7th-grade homeroom teacher. I was so happy that she was my teacher because she was one of the *other* nicest teachers in the school.

In the lunchroom one school day, I heard some teachers in a heated discussion, basically arguing. One of them was insisting that there was still good in whatever student they were talking about. They said that the student could be helped with the right guidance.

Mrs. McMillion, my math and language arts teacher, and Mrs. Walker were the main two teachers who were going back and forth.

Later that day, I'm not sure what I did but I guess I did something to trigger Mrs. McMillion to get angry. She looked me in my face and said to me, "You know little girl, it really takes a *mother* to love you." And to this day, I still remember how her words made me feel.

It felt like my whole existence dropped to my feet. I didn't really know what those words meant at the time, but I *did* know that I didn't like the feeling it gave me. And I also knew that I never wanted anyone to feel this way towards me *ever* again!

After hearing this statement from her, I knew that I was the student she and Mrs. Walker were arguing about.

At the end of this same school day, while running through the school getting into trouble *once again*, Mrs. Robinson grabbed my shirt and pulled me into the corner of a classroom.

She looked me straight in my eyes and said, "Get ahold of yourself! You are NOT who they say you are! I decree and declare in your life that you *will* be different! You will *rise above the ordinary*!"

This confirmed what I already thought the argument was about. Then, I felt like crying, but I held in my tears.

I could tell from the expression on her face and her tone of voice that she believed every word she said.

If only *I* believed her words too.

Nothing about me really changed after this though.

As the "first lady," I held up my end of the school side of things, making sure everyone was on point in recruiting more female gang members and making sure they were well versed in their lit and knowledge.

Before the school year ended, I had recruited over 20 girls, and I was now the leader of them. But I was smart enough to know that these girls were not my friends and that they only respected me out of fear.

I calmed down a *lot* this year though. And, in doing so, I became friends with Mattie and some more students in my class. We became so tight – Fanta, Mattie, Keisha, and Angel. I loved these girls like they were my blood sisters!

My friends kept me out of a lot of trouble. But trouble still found its way to me because of my involvement with my gang.

I was still being arrested for mob action and assault and battery. And I didn't make things any easier on my grandmother either. But, in my defense, I didn't have a clue about this until I met one of the people my grandmother was working for.

My grandmother was a homemaker. One of her clients told me, "Your grandmother loves and cares about you, but you have to chill before you make her lose her job. The constant calling off of work because she has to go to the school for you or leave work to come get you out of lockup is about to get her fired."

I felt horrible! I hadn't realized how my bad behavior was causing issues for my grandmother at her job.

The more I hung out with my new girls/sisters, the more different I became. I was much calmer and focused on what teenagers need to be focused on.

After leaving one of my friend's house, Kesha, I decided to walk through the land where Damone hung out.

As I approached the block, I heard a friend/fellow gang member of ours whistle "Heads up!" He was giving Damone a warning that I was coming.

I looked across the street and saw him sitting on the porch. And sitting between his legs sat a girl holding a baby in her arms.

My heart dropped! I couldn't believe what I was seeing.

He came off the porch and met me halfway up the block. He told me, "Go back the other way."

I asked, "Why ?"

He said, "Because I don't want you to walk that way. I'll come see you when I get a chance."

Now, it didn't take a rocket scientist to figure out that the baby was his and the girl was his girlfriend. I felt REJECTED again!

Finding My Way

Well, I'm in 8th grade and it's graduation time. I am hoping to stay out of trouble to be eligible to attend my graduation.

It was the first week of school when my auntie Leadora and my daddy came to the house for a visit. I loved seeing them both, especially my auntie because we were pretty close.

She used to come visit and pick me up sometimes when I was living with my mom.

Daddy and Auntie Leadora found me in the kitchen frying trout and cooking sauerkraut for my grandmother. (Remember, cooking was a stress reliever for me; so, I cooked often.) I was 14 at the time.

My aunt told me, "Your daddy needs to talk to you."

With my aunt standing behind me, my dad said, "I love you, baby girl. Your daddy is sick. I got HIV."

I remember my legs buckling a little, but I quickly braced myself and I didn't show any emotions. Then my body tensed up as I was trying to hold back the tears while listening to my aunt explain to me what having HIV meant. She made sure I knew everything I needed to know about this disease.

After they left the kitchen, I went into the food pantry and cried.

I couldn't believe I finally made it – 2 months left before graduation!

Other students were deciding on what high school they would attend, so I started doing the same.

I remembered that my auntie Yolanda and Nikki went to Richards High School; and now, so did one of my good friends, Angie. So, cool! I decided, "I will go to Richards with Angie!"

I was so excited and applied to attend Richards. But, instead, I received a letter stating that I was not accepted to attend this school. *Rejection* consumed me all over again now and I needed to release this anger.

Soon after this, I reconnected with some of my *old* friends and decided to attend school with them at Tilden High School.

At this point, I felt I couldn't do any better and this is where I deserve to be… in one of the worst schools in Chicago. But over the next couple of months, I didn't feel too encouraged.

Well, I soon received a rejection letter from Tilden High School. The letter stated that "due to your history of violence and gang affiliation, the school board is concerned your life and safety may be in jeopardy if you were to attend Tilden High School."

WOW! I hadn't realized the dangers of the behaviors I displayed throughout my time in grammar school. Many others were worse off than I was though. Even the ones I banged hard with were able to get into this school. What was wrong with me?

But, now that I'm older, I know that it was all a part of God's plan.

I remember thinking about how I began this year with a new attitude and how proud my grandmother was that she was able to get me out of grammar school.

I remember my grandmother going all out to make sure I looked nice for my graduation. Usually, Easter was the only time I would wear a dress or dress up. I was known as a diehard tomboy. So, wearing a fitted dress that showed my curvy hips and big legs caused mouths to drop and people's faces looked stunned. Even the teachers and principal were shocked!

I was an athlete throughout my days at John Hope. I was on the basketball team playing power forwards. I was good and played one hell of a defense, more so than I played on offense. I protected the ball. And I could play *any* sport: football, softball, tennis, and gymnastics.

RISE ABOVE THE ORDINARY: The Life Behind Her Smile

Englewood High School was the school I was forced to attend because this school was the only school that would accept me. But what I couldn't understand was how the rest of my friends who lived on the same block I lived on were able to go to Tilden, but I couldn't go to Tilden.

I remember when I signed up for a career course when I applied to attend Richards, I chose Home Economics as my career major to follow my other friend. So, when my counselor placed me at Englewood, she signed me up for the same Home Economics course as my career course.

But I wasn't interested in taking Culinary Arts at this school. I thought I would just keep the career course as Home Economics for now, and then change it later. What I didn't know is I was making a temporary choice for what would be a permanent situation because it was God ordained.

During this time, I was only interested in finding out who from my crew was attending Englewood High School with me, what kind of backup did I have, and who was in charge of this school so I could become acquainted and find out my part of the assignments and duties while attending this school as it relates to me submitting under the authority of the school.

But, to my surprise, I soon realized that this school was an opp (opposing gang). This school was covered by another gang that was right in the middle of a different gang. So, there was no rulership for my particular gang of girls. There were only a few of us, so we decided to join in with the males.

They knew who we were and the "seats" (positions in the gang) in which we came from. So, my responsibility now was to keep my ears to the ground to learn information and inform everyone if there was an attack coming.

The day comes when I meet my division teacher; she is also my Culinary Arts teacher. In her introduction of herself to the class, she shared that this was her first-year teaching in the Chicago Public School System and that she spent most of her career in CNA (Corporate America).

I didn't give much attention to her because I just knew that I wasn't staying in this class; again, this was a temporary situation in my mind.

This first year of school was all about finding my way. High School was different: there was more freedom here and a different style of people. There was a lot of school spirit, and the school was crowded.

This actually reminded me of how I viewed high school when I saw it on TV. There were kids sitting at tables with their friends, school jackets that displayed the sports they were a part of, stylish shoes, juke boxes playing on the televisions around the cafeteria, a spades game going in the corner, dice-playing in the other corner, and the noise level super loud.

CHAPTER 8

Tapping into the wrong outlet can and will drain your strength.

LPH

TURNS AND SHIFTS FOR BETTER

TURNS AND SHIFTS FOR BETTER

I remember that, although I was now in high school, I was still willing to put my all into the gang organization that I had been a part of for so many years.

I planned to survey the land: look and see "Who's Who," how they're moving, *who* they're moving with, study the language, who's their opposition, how bad the situation is, who's the connect, who's the leader, what's my role, who do I report to, how to become established, how do I become better, who do I need to hurt to show that I'm here and I'm tougher and fearless.

Mainly how do I keep any spot I gain from being taken?

Damone was not there with me, but I wasn't afraid, although I felt unsafe and unprotected.

Yes, I still have fellow "soldiers" around and they would fight with me, but my protection was Damone, and he is not here.

Loyal to my flag, loyal to the colors, and loyal to what I rep 'd, I found myself consumed with cares for what made me respected instead of cares for the promises I made to my siblings.

I became better at any assignment given to me - from sneaking guns into the school, to holding *pounds* of weed in my locker to being the "watchman" when gang fights popped off.

I was losing myself.

My tone in my step changed. I walked harder and more thuggishly. My attitude was changing, becoming disrespectful to adults, and not caring about getting caught or getting arrested. And I was leading at a bigger level now.

In high school, because I couldn't bring any attention to myself and what I was doing, I had to keep a lot of what I was involved in away from Mattie and Tekesha. I didn't want them involved by knowing anything which may backfire on them some day. I wanted to protect them.

My friends and I became so close that we wouldn't and couldn't be separated. We told each other everything and we did everything together as best friends would do.

Often, I thought about telling them what I was doing but didn't. Somehow, Tekesha eventually found out what I was doing and what was going on, but never told me she knew. But I could tell that she knew.

Soon Damone wasn't consuming my mind as much, and I was making it in the streets on my own.

Since the Chef in the Culinary Arts/Home Economics class had just started teaching, I didn't take her seriously because she was just as new as I was.

Most of the class was filled with my opposition, so I did more watching than learning. I had to keep my ears and eyes open and make sure I was in the center of their talk.

The introduction subject of our cooking class was Sanitation, which made the class very boring to me, so I started cutting her class.

After multiple absences, the Chef asked to speak with me about my attendance in her class, and my defensive wall went up as she came to me with this out of nowhere.

Survive Is My Plan

I told her, "You aren't a good teacher, and you don't know what you are doing. Even your makeup is funny-looking." I figured that I would try hurting her first, and did, so that she wouldn't get the chance to hurt me with her words.

To live and survive in Englewood is a blessing and a curse. If you have a crew or a big family, you're good; but if you don't, sometimes walking and being identified as someone from Englewood could be one of the worst things to happen to you.

What makes a teen an at-risk youth is one whose chances at a successful transition to adult life are hindered by certain circumstances or factors experienced during their childhood.

As a young girl facing multiple factors, you will have a more challenging time growing academically and maturing socially.

I was a child with a learning disability; therefore, the learning disability is a factor that, by itself or in conjunction with another, contributes to my being identified as at risk. This label was outside of my control as a child.

Then there are environmental factors that impact my mental and physical health. What makes this significant is the lasting impact on my ability to function in society and take responsibility for my life.

After finding myself in a school I was forced to attend, I couldn't participate in the school I chose due to my gang background. I was completely isolated from the female crew that I was used to. Therefore, I had to run with other people I didn't know, or trust would have my back.

Fights were breaking out everywhere, and yes, I found myself involved in most of them…with the guys and the girls. These fights were way more intense and dangerous than I had seen in my last school. This was way different.

My sophomore year is here. Although I was involved in trouble time after time, I found myself enjoying my Culinary Arts class and Chef. She turned out to be down to earth. Still prissy, but there was something about her once she dropped the "Let me be professional" act.

Being in the center of classroom conversation, I started developing friendships with some of my classmates without even noticing.

I already knew how to cook, so the class wasn't hard. But I became more interested in the things I didn't learn in my grandmother's kitchen like temperature control, and measuring (grandma measured off of intuition, not ounces.).

One day, Chef approached me as I was on my way to a gang fight. She had heard about the fight and knew I would be involved; so, she waited for me to pass by her classroom door.

She told me, "If you want to continue to be a part of my cooking program, you have to choose, right now, cooking or the gang."

What she did was challenge me to make a choice: keep doing what I was doing, which was an endless road, or choose to do what was a sure road to broaden my horizons and cause me to live.

Back then, you couldn't just say you were in a particular gang; you had to be proven. There was literature to be learned, and if you were caught not knowing it, there were repercussions. I knew my literature and what my gang represented and used it to my advantage to get out.

So that I wouldn't be tempted or pressured to go back, God made it so that my assigned region was abolished from female gangs. We could stay where we were without activity, representation/help, or follow another set in a different location.

Needless to say, I stayed where I was. And no one from the opposite gang ever bothered me.

Before making the critical decision to leave my flag, my colors, and my crew, I went into a very high-profile peace-treaty meeting called by both principals - Dr Brown and Dr Rose - who were former gang leaders themselves.

This peace-treaty meeting was held in the school's gymnasium during school hours. So, there were innocent students and teachers in the building and in their classrooms.

The meeting consisted of gang governors, regions, first ladies, and foot soldiers from both sides. Let me tell you that *this* meeting was so dangerous until, if anything would have gone wrong, the story would have made national news!

I thought I was tough with my crew until I saw these first ladies that were older than I was come in with their crew. Fierce, hard-core, and stepped just as hard as any of the men there. Packing with weapons, some of the first ladies even had blades in their mouth!

For the first time, I saw what I could become in this lifestyle, a lifestyle I admired and thought I wanted.

Thoughts started entering my mind, like "What if someone in here says the wrong thing or makes the wrong move? What would and could happen?"

I didn't like this feeling I was feeling. I felt so unprotected! None of the big people knew who I was.

My crew didn't attend Englewood; therefore, I was merely a "simp" who governed the lookout crew amongst the crowd of gang leaders who covered territories.

But something was telling me that it was meant for me to be in this meeting. And I was having some serious thoughts as I looked at Sonya and her girls scan the audience for threats: "Is this the kind of woman I wanted to become?"

While my girl Chanel was sitting next to me, my mind started wandering, and every word of Chef's challenge entered my thoughts. Then followed the vision of my last encounter with Damone sitting on the porch with the girl and the baby.

Mrs. McMillion's words I could hear clearly now, "It takes a mother to love you!" Then flows in the promise I made to my siblings, and then came the guilt I felt because I forgot about the promise once again through my actions, and because I wanted to stay in my gang.

But something stronger was pushing me to choose my family.

With all these thoughts coming at once, I felt taunted, and my head was overloaded and about to burst! I couldn't get the thoughts out of my head "Just run away and forget everything and everybody…just run!!"

These were my final thoughts before I came to myself. Then, I was angry, and I faulted God.

A Chicago Tribune columnist who also worked at Englewood High School knew of my actions and gang run in and listed me as one of the worst teenage gang members on the Southside, stating that I "would not live to see age 18 at the rate I was going."

This article angered me so much! I was thinking, "This is not who I really am! And (most importantly) I cannot die out here! I have to save my sisters and brothers before they are lost in the system, and no one can find them!"

Here is the beginning of a new dawning.

The weight of Chef's challenge was pretty heavy. So, I decided to make Culinary Arts more of my focus. I told Chef, "I will be committed to your class, but you will have to hold me accountable to keeping my word."

Now, the rest of the year was filled with making new friends and playing every sport. I was the captain of the bowling, softball, tennis, and girls' basketball teams; and, of course, I was learning more about Culinary Arts and Hospitality in their entirety.

Good Days Got Better

The Chef and I had become very close, like for real mother and daughter. This lady was hilariously funny! And when she found out that I believed in God, she instantly invited me to church.

She would take me to church with her, and sometimes to her home to keep me accountable and from being tempted to do any of the things I used to do in my past.

She really broadened my horizons in business and follow-up.

Her sons accepted me as their little sister and her husband accepted me as his "bonus" daughter.

I would stay late after school to assist Chef with whatever she was doing to prepare the classroom for the next school day.

She would stay late after school until I finished with sports; then, she would drop me off at home.

This went on non-stop for 2 years and became a routine.

My actions had changed, and my grades had changed, holding a 2.5 GPA. So, I thought that maybe now I could transition out of the IEP that was based on my learning disability.

My disposition had changed, I became known all over the school for my cooking and sports, and teachers were now invested in me.

They kept me out of trouble by allowing me to practice my Culinary Arts skills during their class time. I could continue training for the competitions that Chef enrolled some of us in as long as I completed my classwork for their classes.

I was going to school meetings with Chef. I listened and learned everything there was to know about the program we were in called Education To Careers (ETC), the cluster classes, and how they worked best for students, Careers To Education strands. I was Chef's mini-me.

All was going well for me: the principal knew my name, and for good reasons this time. I was mentioned throughout the news column as a "rising star" in the Culinary industry and in the school newspaper.

I felt free and I felt loved by people who were *not* my mother. Our Culinary Arts Class Division 711 was like family. We did everything together and we had all of our classes together.

It's now my junior year of high school and it's basketball season. Chef had never been to one of my games before because she didn't like sports, so I invited/begged her to come, and she agreed.

We played Carver High School for this game that I invited Chef to. I was so excited that she was finally coming to see me play!

I was a good forward, which was the position I played. The game started and I noticed Chef in the corner standing by the bleachers in her lab coat. Then, right after the game started, I saw her leave. And she never returned to the gym.

I thought, "Why wouldn't she stay for my game? Why couldn't she support me?"

During halftime, I ran to her classroom, which was not far from the gymnasium, to see if she was okay. As I approached her classroom, I saw that she was fine: she was in the classroom talking and laughing with other teachers.

Right then, something so heavy fell upon me. My heart was hurting because all sorts of emotions were swallowing me whole as I walked back into the gymnasium to continue playing with my team.

School Riot On Me

The second half of the game had begun, and the girls from the opposing team had been trash-talking and hacking me the entire first half of the game. I ignored her and brushed her off before, but *now*... not so much.

The more she talked, the angrier I became.

I warned her that, if she kept it up, I was going to get her at the end of the game. But she never stopped. So, as I promised, I walked over to the girl and punched her in her face. I was so *angry*.

As I tried to keep her from running up the bleachers away from me, one of her teammates jumped in and hit me in the back with a crutch.

Before you knew it, the entire Englewood basketball team and spectators ran over to help me fight. But I was out of control and so angry that I never felt the pain of being hit with a crutch.

No one could control me...at least not until one of the teammates' mom, who was big and muscular, grabbed me in a bear hug.

As I tried to escape her grip, she yelled, "STOP Kisha, STOP!!!!... Just stop and calm down. Take a deep breath and calm down."

Moments later, I was calm...Faith (the teammate's mom), while still holding me in the bear hug, turned me around, and said, "Now, look!"

I calmed down, came to myself, and looked around the gym at what was going on. It seemed as if everything I was seeing was in slow motion. *Everyone* was fighting. And the people were out of control. Guys hitting girls, and kids were fighting the coach from the other team. I couldn't believe what was happening! *And* I couldn't believe that I started this riot. The entire 61st Street police station was in the gym breaking up fights.

Fear came over me...I was sad, and my mind was taking over once again.

I *knew* I hadn't changed because every negative thought came flooding back into my mind. And now I have proven that everything that was said about me is true.

My ugliness had shown itself once again, and the unlovable Kisha was back. But I will escape it!

I prayed, "GOD, I tried to change! I thought you *healed* me from this person!"

This is when I understand the meaning of this passage of scripture: *"For the good that I would I do not: but the evil which I would not, that I do. I find then a law, that, when I would do good, evil is present with me."* Romans 7:19, 21

So, I understand that total and complete deliverance of *some* areas in life comes through the process of time. And the absence of that level of deliverance does not invalidate me or my salvation.

LAKISHA P HUNTER

CHAPTER 9

Coming up as a young adult I didn't trust myself because I had no frame of reference.

LPH

YET LIFE KEEPS LIFE-IN'

LAKISHA P HUNTER

YET LIFE KEEPS LIFE-IN'

I remember that, after the fight, needless to say, there were major consequences for my actions with fighting Carver High School. I was arrested and sent home to wait for the decision to be made for expulsion.

I had no idea that I was going to be expelled from school.

I remember thinking, "Why did I get *this* angry at Chef for not staying longer for my game? She's my teacher, not my mother. She didn't sign up for the embarrassment and troubles I'm causing her."

Chef did not speak to me for a while, but she at school fighting for my life. She went to each teacher who had taught me over the past 3 years and asked them to write a letter to the principal on my behalf about the improvements I had made and my transition.

Every teacher that Chef asked wrote the letter, including some who had not taught me but watched from afar!

It *still* wasn't looking good though. The school was on academic probation already to the point where there were teams from the board of education put in place to help turn the school around. Therefore, I was to be made an example out of.

However, when it came time to expel me, the decision instead was made in my favor: since I had an IEP due to a learning disability, I could *not* be expelled from school. Instead, I was placed on probation with an action plan and make to take anger management classes after school (which was created for students like me) to correct my behavior.

When I returned to school after being gone for several days, I was very quiet and stayed to myself.

After the basketball fight, I was banned from playing sports for the rest of the school year.

Chef was so relieved that I was not kicked out of school. I was too!

During the rest of this year, I focused on making money by writing resumes for my peers. I learned how to write a resume in Culinary when Chef taught the Hospitality Management section of the assigned class books - National Restaurant Association Education Foundation ProStart books.

I actually still use this book today when I'm teaching youth and as a reference to refresh my knowledge and sharpen my skills.

Now, I found myself leaning on the hospitality side of Culinary more than cooking. There's something intriguing about treating people special and making people feel good. Being kind to people and turning bad experiences into the greatest experience ever is nothing short of masterful!

Not everyone can master this skill because it's not about the skill itself; it's about the genuineness in the skill. Genuineness is a quality that no one can fake, and *authenticity* is my DNA.

I made so much money writing resumes and cover letters until I could have opened a Resume Business.

Chef showed me the type of paper to use for the resumes, and I was able to charge extra due to the quality of the paper. The money I made was enough to buy myself some "hipper" clothes and shoes and keep up with the latest hairstyles - my cousin LaDonna kept my hair on point!

I was grateful for my cousin LaDonna because, when I couldn't afford to get my hair done, she'd do my hair anyway without charging me. She didn't like charging me anyway, but I understood that she had bills and kids to take care of like adults did.

So, I was chill now. I was doing well again, and I was looking at life from a different lens. I liked doing good, and I liked people looking forward to eating my cooking and enjoying it.

Chef would allow me to bake cookies in the lab, and I would sell out of them all on my lunch break.

Life Back At Home

On the home front: during my junior year of high school, I was dating Jamie Sails (aka Chicago).

At this time, it was nice outside; I'm not sure of the season, but I decided to take the bus over to the Eastside of Chicago where I had visited Jamie before.

He and I always had fun when we were together; he was a prankster. We both were in ROTC in school, and his plan was to go to the army.

Jamie lived with his foster mom, and she didn't like me. "She's too dark." she told him.

This time when I went to visit Jamie, I stayed a little too long to the point where I had missed the last bus that would take me back to the southwest side (Englewood). Jamie and I waited at the bus stop for over an hour before realizing the weekend bus schedule was in effect.

Jamie walked me back to his house so I could call my grandmother to tell her what happened. I told her that I did not know how to get home, and the last bus was at 8:00pm due to the weekend hours. I had no idea about the bus schedule because this was my first time visiting on a weekend.

My grandmother was livid! Once she comes up with her own version of what really happened in a situation, there was no convincing her otherwise.

Amid her curse words, she said, "If you don't make it home by midnight, I'm gone beat you!" Then she yelled, "You stayed late on purpose! You knew what you were doing with yo' fast ass!"

Jamie shared the situation with his foster mother, but she would not take me home.

So, I called my grandmother back to explain to her once again that I had no way home.

And, amid her calling me "little fast bitch and hoe," she yelled, "You just wanted to stay the night to have sex! You gone be like yo' nasty-ass momma with a lot of kids!"

I just held the phone and listened. After we hung up, I went upstairs to Jamie's room to go to sleep.

But *every* word my grandmother spoke was ringing in my ears.

I couldn't believe that she would think I'd do something like this on purpose. I had never done anything like this before, and I would never disrespect my grandmother in this way.

Jamie did his best to make me comfortable, but nothing worked. Eventually, we cuddled under the covers. But then, the closer he got to me, the more I became aware of what he wanted to do.

He rubbed my back, my thighs, and my arm. He kissed the back of my neck, then he whispered in my ear, "Can we?"

I truly dreaded him asking this question. I said, "I don't want to." So, he stopped.

Then, he began again moments later, but I stood my ground.

He asked, "Why not?"

I said, "My grandmother thinks I stayed too late on purpose because she thinks I wanted to have sex with you and that isn't what happened."

He replied, "Well, she thinks it anyway. So, you might as well."

I said, "Then, I would be proving her right. I am *not* what she called me, and I did not do this on purpose. Therefore, it's a No."

He didn't ask again. He just held me in his arms until we both fell asleep.

Home For The Holidays

Thanksgiving in my grandmother's house was always she-and-I time. But I didn't like it initially because I have to wake up too early to help cook. But, during the Christmas holiday, my mom and dad would come to visit.

Aunts and uncles came from all their hiding places and rocks they were under all year and made their way to Grandma's house.

Music played throughout the house, Jack Daniel's was in my grandmother's glass, and beer for momma and daddy to drink as usual.

My stepdad would come too. All were welcome! Grownups bussed jokes, and there was dancing and reminiscing.

Older cousins played spades while the teens would hang around the cousins catching what we can catch to learn what we could about what's going on throughout the family. We were all reminiscing on the sneaky times and behaviors too.

While I enjoyed being with my family, I still missed my other half - the 4 younger siblings.

One year when we went to visit my younger siblings, Stephanie wanted to sneak out of the center by trying to hide under my grandmother's dress. This broke all of our hearts.

After a while, times became hard for my grandmother as she could not get out of the house as much because her knees were worsening - she had arthritis in both of her knees. So, sometimes we went *months* without seeing my siblings because of my grandmother's difficulty with getting out of the house.

Time For School Again

It was the beginning of the school year of 1994, and the adults around the neighborhood knew of my bad reputation for fighting and gangbanging, so they feared for the safety of their children if they were to hang with me.

I remember walking down past one of my friends' house on 56th and Carpenter streets, which was just a block away from where I lived . Her grandmother was sitting on her front porch and beckoned for me to come to the porch where she was. I looked around wondering if she was talking to me.

Then she yelled from across the street again, "Little girl! Come here!"

As my crew and I walked toward her to see what she wanted, she said to my crew, "Y'all stay where you are. I didn't ask for you."

Then I said to my crew, "Fall back." and proceeded to the porch.

She said, "I know who you are. I'm Mrs. Robert's, Courtney's grandmother, and I don't want you hanging around with my granddaughter."

I couldn't say a word because I would never disrespect an adult. That was a *big* no-no and frowned upon by all.

She went on to ask me, "Who is your mother? Where is she?"

I replied, "I live with my grandmother."

She replied, "I'm sure that your grandmother would be disappointed if she knew of all this fighting and gangbanging you're doing out here."

Still in shock at the nerves of this lady, seeing that I take up for and protect her granddaughter. But of course, she didn't know all of that.

She finally said, "Stop your behavior. Focus on being a little girl and not a hoodlum."

Now, these words didn't stop me from hanging with Courtney; but I didn't hang with her at home.

But later in that same year, some classmates of mine wanted to fight Courtney. One of the girl's family was a part of the same gang I was in. One day these girls wanted to fight Tekesha and Courtney for something silly – over a boy!

So, they tried to jump Courtney on this bus stop. Then, they proceeded to follow Tekesha, Mattie, and myself on our route home. When we reached 63rd and Halsted streets, the fighting commenced between Tekesha and the girls. But there was no way I wasn't going to help Tekesha.

Amongst the other girls were Porsha, Kelly, Monique, Ella, and big Ella. And Ella was a force! We used to fight together; I mean, beat down *dudes* when gang fights broke out. We would bang side by side. But on this day, because I was no longer plugged in with the crew, she felt she needed to help the others whose family was affiliated.

That was the biggest bunch of bull I had ever heard!

Ella hit me so hard that I couldn't see what I was doing. We all were fighting until eventually we ran off. There were 5 of them against the 3 of us.

But I was furious! I couldn't believe I got jumped on for the 1st time ever. And jumped by girls who I thought I was cool with - my culinary classmates. They all have been to my house. And one actually dated my uncle Cortez and spent nights over at my house too. So, I was not going to allow them to get away with this.

For the first time ever, I told my grandmother about this fight. She couldn't believe that these same girls who had been to her house and hung out with my family jumped on me.

By this time, I see my sister Falisha. She runs to me and tells me, "Kelly, Porsha, and Monique chased me home!"

Now, this means war! I went to my uncle's hiding place and got his gun. He had shown me where his gun was in the event he ever needed me to bring it to him.

Tekesha and I walked to Monique's grandmother's house, and I had the gun in my sweater. When we reached the block before the house, we saw all 3 of them on the back porch talking loudly about the fight. So, we stopped and watched them.

I was so angry until I planned out in my head how this was going to go. Watching them from afar, they didn't have a clue that we were standing by watching them.

I pulled the gun from underneath my sweater and the bullets fell out of the gun. The cylinder on the revolver was very loose because it was broken. I had no idea! And I was so mad until I could scream!!

Therefore, we decided to get them later.

About an hour later, Tekesha and her boyfriend picked me up in his car. She's in the front, and I'm in the back of the car - Chevy with tented windows.

He took us to the store where big Ella was hanging out. We pulled up right next to her and she had no idea what was about to happen.

We watched and analyzed the situation. Tekesha's boyfriend asked, "What do y'all want to do?"

I wanted so badly to hurt her where she stood because I was so hurt. We were so close! But I knew, if we fought her that we would have to watch our backs or we would literally have to take her out. So, we decided to leave.

But what came to mind as they were taking me home is that people really don't know that their lives can be taken just like that; and over something so senseless! And that three times today lives could have been taken and the people had no idea.

Let me tell you why I say three times.

To my surprise, what I didn't know until I got back home with the gun was my uncle Cortez was mad, I mean mad as *hell* at me!

He told me, "That gun is broken! And if you had fired it, the gun would have backfired and possibly shot you in the face!"

I immediately dropped the gun on the floor and prayed, "God, I thank You that I didn't pull the trigger !"

Someone Speaks For Me

The next day, we went to school. And I cut Chef's class so that the girls who jumped me would think I didn't come to school. Tekesha and I had planned our revenge. We waited outside Chef's classroom for the girls to walk out. And, whoever came out first was getting jumped.

My basketball coach was just walking by when the bell rang.

Out comes Monique first. I never gave her a chance to realize what was about to happen.

She looked at me like everything was cool though; like jumping me never happened.

That's when I hit her. And I hit her so hard until her eye started bleeding. The fight was a heads up. Tekesha didn't need to jump.

And even with Chef yelling, "STOP! STOP! STOP!" I couldn't stop, and I wouldn't stop charging at her.

Coach Henderson came and grabbed me and held me against the wall. And other security ran to assist him.

Then, I'm thinking to myself, "This is it! I know I'm in trouble now. I know I'm getting kicked out."

We were all sent to the principal's office, even Courtney. The school called our parents, but my grandmother couldn't leave work to come get me.

After Mrs. Roberts was done letting the principal have it, she told Courtney, "Come on!" And seeing me still sitting there, she told them, "And I'm the parental consent for her as well."

Needless to say, I was shocked. This lady didn't like me. But she heard that the reason I was fighting initially was because I was protecting her granddaughter.

Monique and her mother tried lying by saying that I hit her with a lock and busted her eye.

But thank God that Coach Henderson saw everything and told the authorities, "She didn't have a weapon. She hit her with her fist."

I was suspended from school. Tekesha and Mattie were not though. So, I put out a warning that, if anyone touched either one of them while I was gone, I was coming back fighting.

When I got home, I just laid across my bed knowing my grandmother would be disappointed once again for getting suspended from school.

When my grandmother came home from work, she asked, "Why you lying in the bed? What's wrong?"

I told her what happened and that I was suspended.

And to my surprise, my grandmother replied, "Well, I'm glad you defended yourself."

I said, "Well grandma, I only got one of them. I have to get one more."

My grandma responded, "They shouldn't have jumped you! Do what you have to do." Then, she said, "Go outside and be home for curfew."

What!! This has never happened before. I was in the right and not the wrong this time?? Oh, what a feeling!

CHAPTER 10

I depended on those who were supposed to be more mature than me for guidance. Most times my kindness was taken advantage of instead.

LPH

I MADE IT IN SPITE OF

LAKISHA P HUNTER

I MADE IT IN SPITE OF

I remember that 1997 was my senior year of high school.

Jamie and I are still in our relationship. And now I have developed very strong feelings for him. But Love wasn't a word I used at all, except with my father Still, I knew it was love that I felt for him and he spoke of the same kind of feeling that he had for me.

RISE ABOVE THE ORDINARY: *The Life Behind Her Smile*

In those days, couples would go to the mini mall on 63rd and Halsted streets to take pictures and get these big buttons made with their pictures on them. So, Jamie and I did as all the high school couples.

Jamie had moved from the far east side with his foster mom to someplace closer to the school with his biological mother and his sister Bobbie. I really liked his mom and sister. We were very close, and they were a lot of fun.

Since my curfew was 8pm every day, I couldn't hang out late because my grandmother was strict with curfew.

So, Jamie and I were doing almost everything that everyone else was doing as a couple except having sex. But he never pressured me to do *anything*, which is why I felt he would have been deserving of it.

So, I caught the bus to his house in the evening, but he wasn't home. His sister Bobbie was home and told me I could find him in a building just around the corner on the 3rd floor.

I hurried around the corner into the building, up to the 3rd floor and knocked on the door excited to see him, but no one answered.

I went back and got Bobby, and she walked me back to the building; then, she knocked on the door. This time Jamie answered the door.

As I leaned in to hug him, a short, dark-skinned girl named Cocoa pulled the for open wider and all I saw was her *huge* belly - she was pregnant!

My stomach dropped to the bottom of my shoes, my heart skipped a beat and my breathing seemed like I couldn't catch my breath.

"Not again!" I'm thinking in my head. The very same thing that happened with Damone is happening to me again?!

But I could not and would not let them see me sweat, or see me hurt, or see me cry, although I was experiencing all of these things inside.

I know that I should have expected this: he was going to be 18 years old, and not having sex with his girlfriend didn't mean that he was not having sex; he was going to get the sex he craved from *somewhere*.

I just stared, said nothing, then I turned and left. And *that* was the end of Jamie and Kisha.

On The Home Front

This is my senior year now, and I realize that this is the time to put what I've learned to work.

I was elected by my peers as the Senior Class President, and I won homecoming queen and winter ball queen.

For the past 2 years, Chef brought in everyone she could think of from the Culinary and Hospitality Industry to teach and train the class on the things she did not know how to do professionally to prepare us for the event that we had all been waiting for - The cooking competition, a culinary competition for CPS Culinary Programs across the city of Chicago.

There were interviews and portfolios we had to prepare and present, along with cutting skills, and cooking and measuring skills; this time of the school year was super intense and a big deal.

There were about 7 of us from Englewood who competed.

I remember doing a great job with the Culinary part of the competition, and my portfolio was immaculate.

During my interview, I had to answer questions about my attendance issues that showed on my school transcript. They all accumulated when I was suspended from school, which resulted in lower grades than normal.

One of the judges asked, "Explain what was happening at that time when your grades were so low."

I explained, "During this time, I was not taking my life seriously. I was involved in gang activity. But, after coaching from my teacher and my love for cooking increased, I turned my life around to pursue my dream of becoming a chef." I continued my explanation, "I have maintained a 2.5 GPA that is currently climbing, and perfect attendance since the 2nd half of my junior year."

One of my good friends and classmates won the highest scholarship offered ($40,000) to Johnson and Wales University); and they were so excited.

Everyone just knew I would get the scholarship to Sullivan or one of the other 2 big scholarships But, instead, I was awarded a $500 scholarship to Lexington Women Business College. My classmates, Chef, and even Culinary teachers from other schools were completely shocked at the outcome.

When talking with the interviewer Mr. Goodman, I remember feeling that I did not fit the image that the founder was looking for to award the bigger scholarships. I remember talking with him about all the things I was involved in and doing to better myself, but he kept this blank expression on his face.

I remember before the final competition, Mr. Goodman did speak to me but did not hold a conversation with me as he did the others. I never thought anything of it seeing that I wasn't really a person who held conversation. I was comfortable with Chef and a few other teachers, but this man's expression did stand out in my mind.

I went to prom and had a great time. And I went to the luncheon where I won all of the awards allowed.

My prom date was a friend of mine from the neighborhood.

Chef and her husband attended and so did my girls. We all looked beautiful. It was a great day for this former tom-boy!

Graduation Is Here!

Just one day to go! My grandmother was so excited about finally getting me across this stage to receive my High School Diploma!

But of course, something bad always had to happen: My aunt Yolanda and I had a huge argument that turned into her hitting me and then we tussled.

I wasn't really hitting my aunt back like I would have had it been someone on the street though. So, what I did was run out of the house and threw a brick through her car windshield.

Yolanda was so mad that she called the police on me. She was looking to press charges against me, so I didn't come back home until late that night when Yolanda had already gone out for the night.

The next morning was graduation day and Yolanda was still pretty upset with me. She still wanted to call the police on me, but my grandmother pleaded with her and begged her not to.

With fury in her voice, Yolanda yelled, "I hate you!" as she went to her room to cry.

My grandmother made me pay for the windshield with my $30 allowance until it was paid in full.

On this same day, I walked around the neighborhood nervous about the trouble I was about to get into about Yolanda's car windshield.

I remember walking past Mrs. Robert's house, but this time I crossed to the opposite side of the street because I didn't want any trouble from this lady today. But as God would have it. Mrs. Roberts, aka *Granny*, called me to her porch once again.

But *this* time she had a different tone in her voice. She asked, "Do you know God?"

I said, "Defensively I know God and I believe in God."

She said, "Well little girl, God told me that He's going to use you one day for His glory."

I didn't know what that meant, but I liked the sound of God making use of me to do something for Him!

Granny went on to say, "Come go to church with me and all my family."

I said, "I will go with you on Sunday."

Now it's time to walk across the stage!

As class president, I had to give a speech before my fellow classmates and graduates. I even presented Chef with a plaque from our Culinary class for all the hard work she poured into her very first class coming into Englewood High School in 1993! She cried like a baby.

My daddy, in all of his soberness for the past 4 years, was in attendance for my graduation. My grandmother, Falisha, and big brother Micheal all came to my graduation too.

But even with a threat on the phone from my grandmother telling my mother she'd better not miss my high school graduation, my mom did not come.

Although I knew in my heart that she wasn't coming, I still looked for her to walk through the door at any moment; but she never did.

I attended Lexington College that fall. Lexington, a catholic college, was located south in the 100's in Chicago.

I was nervous, but I adjusted quickly.

There were only 3 other blacks in this school with me. It was a small and intimate setting of a school. The financial aid department helped me get more money through donors and federal funding to pay for the rest of my tuition.

Life was changing right before my eyes! My community was becoming larger the more I stayed away from negativity.

I remember waking up in a panic the Sunday after my 18th birthday. I had the unction to go to find a church. It was such an urgency. I got dressed and had Chef come pick me up for church.

But when the preacher gave the invitation to join, I'd always freeze. Emotionally I wanted to go but spiritually I didn't know if I should.

The next Sunday I didn't call Chef, but I woke up with the same unctioning and visited a church that was in the neighborhood. It was kind of a big church, but I didn't like all the showboating that I saw. It just didn't feel good. So, I left before the end of service.

I had gotten frustrated but then I remembered the church granny invited me to - Zion Temple. So, the next

Sunday, I went down to Granny's house and asked if I could go to church with her and her family.

This church was a very good fit for me. The frustration and anxiety were gone. I felt comfortable and I understood what the preacher was saying. I was able to follow and keep up. I felt at home here.

So, I joined my very 1st church that Sunday - Zion Temple Missionary Baptist Church.

CHAPTER 11

Strength is made perfect when you know where to place it!

LPH

A LOVE LIKE DADDY'S

A LOVE LIKE DADDY'S

I remember hearing it said many times and in many ways that a girl seeks a man who is just like her father.

Graduation has come and gone, and I just turned 18 years old. I finally found a church God sent me to and I'm loving it!

I started college and I'm officially a grown woman.

I began to think to myself, "What does this really mean for me? What does this change?"

RISE ABOVE THE ORDINARY: The Life Behind Her Smile

While riding to class on the red-line train, I bumped into a familiar face from the neighborhood - his name is Rico.

I was hoping he didn't see or recognize me because he often had something negative to say to me whenever he saw me walking in the neighborhood. And sometimes he would throw rocks at me. I used to avoid him at *all* costs. I used to think, "Why does he always bother me?"

Rico and his 2 best friends were always together. You didn't see one without the other. They were 3 of the most sought-after guys in the neighborhood: well-dressed, good-looking, and wearing the freshest and most up-to-date gear. They were the stuff.

But this Rico guy just wouldn't leave me alone. I'd play basketball with my uncle and some more guys in the alley, and he'd be there watching the game with his other buddies yelling, "Girls can't hoop!" And I couldn't *stand* this guy, but I never said anything back to him.

While sitting across from him on the train, he spoke to me. He asked me, "Where you been? I haven't seen you in a while."

I was thinking, "He's actually being nice to me?! That's different from what I thought he would do!"

Rico kept talking, telling me that he was heading or coming from work. But I don't know exactly what he said because I was busy trying to mind my business and wished his stop would come soon.

Before we parted ways on the train, he asked me, "Can I have your number or come by your house to see you?

In disbelief of what he had asked, I replied "Yeah right!"

He laughed, and said, "Naw, I'm serious."

I continued to disregard his gestures, saying to him, "I remember you always throwing rocks at me. What grown man does *that*?!... Aaand, you always made fun of me playing basketball!" While I was talking, I was thinking in my head that there's *no way* he would want to come see *little, regular* me…he can get any girl from around the way!

He laughed and said " I was just trying to get your attention. I like you and I had to wait 'til the time was right to approach you."

As I exited the train he yelled "See you later! I'll be to see you around 6pm."

I said, "Ok." But I didn't take him seriously at all.

Walking from the train station to the bus stop, I thought of my siblings and immediately sadness came over me.

It had been months since I last saw them. Either my grandmother or Yolanda couldn't take us, or their foster parents wouldn't bring them.

This one older woman named Allie Mae Bishop took in all 4 of my sisters and brothers. She was not a woman who held her tongue. She admitted to not wanting them to see us; and for us to not come to her house to visit them and they couldn't visit us. She felt that, because of her past experiences with other foster kids, we would taint or corrupt them, causing more harm than good to them.

I remember her saying, "This won't work."

But she had no idea how we were raised or my family. My grandmother didn't raise disrespectful girls, and we obeyed adults. So, we would never tell them to do something outside of what they're told to do.

Evening came, before heading down to granny's house to visit Courtney, I stopped at home to check in with my grandmother. She shared with me that a boy came looking for me.

A few names came to mind, but this boy who came looking for me wasn't any of the ones I gave; therefore, I didn't have a clue as to who that could have been.

Later that night, around 8pm, I was walking home, and I heard someone call my name from afar. It was Rico!

I was surprised to see him!

He said, "I just came from your house looking for you! And I came by earlier too, but your grandmother said you weren't home."

"Oh, wow!" I said. "That was YOU that my grandmother was saying came by?! Oh Lord! I forgot, and I didn't believe you when you said you were coming."

He said, "Well, I'm glad I see you now."

We continued talking, about what I don't remember.

"Come take a walk with me." he said.

"Where?" I asked.

He said, "It's kind of cool out. So, we can walk to my house 3 blocks away."

With neck rotation and attitude, "I am not going to your house!"

He asked, "Why not?"

"Because there's nothing for me at your house. *That's why!* I'm not that girl."

He said, "I know who you are, and you don't have to be afraid. I'm not going to do anything to you."

I said, "No way, and I'm going home!" I left him standing right on the corner of the block of 56th and Carpenter streets.

I was so *furious* when I got home. I was thinking to myself, "I *knew* he was a fake and a phony! He only wants to get in my panties and tell all of his friends. Nope, not me! Not today or ever!"

In the next several days, Rico was determined to prove that he wasn't on anything foolish. And he did eventually and won me over.

Four months had passed of us seeing one another, and I saw that he was not at all who I thought he was.

We talked about *everything*, and he kept a smile on my face. He was so silly and fun to be around! And I've never felt these feelings I'm feeling for him.

Yet, I still had some hesitation because dating him was still unreal to me. "Why me?" I wondered.

Moving Forward For Life

In May 1998, the NRA's (National Restaurant Association) show was at McCormick Place. And I was asked to work for one of the vendors at the show.

While there and on my lunch break, I was able to walk around and visit other vendors.

I looked forward to the NRA show every year, with all the different food tastings, new gadgets, and new creative equipment for commercial restaurants and at-home kitchens.

This is my first year working at the show, and this year I met a man from Nigeria - He was young and rich. He was in a booth at the show. I do not remember what products his company was showcasing, but he was different. He sat towards the back of the booth watching everyone and everything.

There was a very young man that stood by his side and the other man spoke for him and the business. When the young, rich man saw me passing by his booth, he rose from his seat and walked over to where I was standing.

He introduced himself as Prince Tumi. He was dressed in a suit, but covered also in a Nigerian scarf that draped his entire body. He was nice to look at, and his skin was so beautiful.

I said, "I'm Lakisha Hunter and I'm in school to become a chef."

We talked for about an hour. Therefore, I was late heading back to relieve the other young lady for her break.

Prince Tumi and one of his men walked me back to the booth. Before leaving, he asked, "Would you be willing to have dinner with me before I leave Chicago?"

I said, "Sure!" and gave him my phone number and address since he offered to pick me up.

I told everyone when I got home about Prince Tumi. My auntie Nikki was my favorite and always told me what to do in dating; and kept my African box braids on point.

The next day was the day I had planned to go to dinner with Prince Tumi.

As my auntie Nikki was finishing my hair, Rico popped up to see me. He came into the living room and then followed me into the washroom since I went in there to look at my hair in the mirror.

As I looked into the mirror, Rico came behind me and wrapped his arm around my waist, kissed my neck, and said, "You look beautiful. I love the braids!"

Looking in the mirror our eyes meet up. And with the purest words I ever heard come out of a man's mouth, and with dreamy eyes, he said to me, "I love you."

If you could have seen the shock on my face!

Besides my daddy and granddad, no man has *ever* said these words to me before. And I knew it was real because of the feeling it gave me. I felt this comfort once before in my childhood, at my grandma's house, from my daddy.

I didn't respond to his words though.

He kissed me on the lips and said, "I'm going downstairs to Renee's house. I'll see you when your aunt is done with the final touches.

Now, I was so caught up on cloud nine with Rico that I forgot about Prince Tumi and our dinner date!

The phone rang, and it was Tumi. "What am I going to do?!" I thought. "This man just confessed his love to me, and I *know* I love him! I'm nowhere *near* interested in Prince Tumi - I just wanted to go to dinner with him. "

Prince Tumi is downstairs ringing my bell. Everyone is looking out the window wondering who the man is that's dressed in a dashiki and riding in a luxury car with his own driver.

Renee runs upstairs and into the living room to see who he was looking for. I told Falisha, "Make sure Rico doesn't look out the window!"

She said, "Too late! We all saw him out the window and heard Nikki and May-May tell him that you are not home."

Renee went to the car to tell Prince Tumi I wasn't home so that Rico couldn't hear. Prince Tumi asked her to relay a message and gave her $20.00 for being willing to give me the message.

At this point, Rico came upstairs into the front room where I was and looked at me with a certain look. If he knew the prince was here for me, he never said that he knew. We just went on with our day.

Real Or Fake Love

All love is not tender, and some love is.

I used to think, "I know my mother loves me because she has to, right? You would think because I'm her child."

When you don't have the balance of these two different kinds of love; when someone shows you love that's different than what you're used to seeing as love, most times you will reject the different love just because you're not used to seeing love in this manner. But you don't know that it in fact really is love.

My mother and others I was around, if not every day, often didn't show love the way my father showed me love. I was disciplined, talked to roughly, called out of my name, and my uncle even named me "Spook" as a pet name because I was dark.

I come from adults tending to their wants and needs first. But my father showed me the love that he wanted me to feel which was the tender kind of love. He *always* told me he loved me, and that I was beautiful. He laughed and played with me. He told me that he would kill someone if they tried to hurt me. He hugged me, he kissed my forehead and cheeks, and he would give me his last.

No, I did not see my dad for years at a time, but he left a great impression of love for me to hold on to until he returned.

I felt he put me first, and he showed me this most when I was 14. He asked me, "Do you want me to stop drinking?"

I said, "Yes."

And he did and never touched drugs or alcohol again.

Now, Rico is giving me the tender kind of love that I was missing in the absence of my daddy; the love that I thought only my father housed for me. I was safe, free, and in love with Rico.

But it's been almost a year and I had not shared these words with him yet. And I don't recall if I've ever used the word verbally towards anyone before.

He never pressured me to say it back though.

When we became more intimate in our relationship, he respected me even more. He hardly asked and never pressured me to be intimate with him. He respected what I was about in church and in pursuing my education.

He told me often, "I will *never* come between your education and your walk with God."

But I never told him that, after being intimate with him, I would feel really bad because I knew I was going against the Bible. I would be thinking, "We are not married. I don't understand why I am so ready and willing!" Then, I would cry myself to sleep because of what I was thinking and doing.

My auntie Nikki talked to me and explained that I was in sexual need (horny) and it was normal and natural.

I was still thinking, "But why do I feel like I am doing something so bad? Why can't I feel *normal* about it like everyone else? This ain't fair, God!"

Rico stopped by to kiss me goodnight this one particular evening. After practicing in the mirror all day, I told Rico during one of our passionate kisses, "I love you." Then, we both cried.

Rico and I were in love and dated for 7 years. Well, we broke up and dated on and off for 7 *more* years. We always found our way back to each other no matter who we were dating otherwise.

Living Life My Way

I finally got to see my sisters and brothers.

Mrs. Allie Mae allowed May-May and I to come and visit in her house in the wild hundreds. It was pretty cool seeing them again, and we were all so excited. I'm not sure why she changed her mind about us visiting, but I'm glad she did.

While going to school, I worked at Englewood High School with the night school. Dr Kidd, the new assistant principal, was very fond of me and hired me as her program manager. I was good at my job and had clout with my former teachers as they had to report to me for questions and answers, grades, and curriculums.

Every 2 weeks when I got paid, I would buy myself fresh gear to match the energy of my man like new shoes and starter jackets. And my cousin Ladonna kept me up with the hottest hairstyles. And I had access to Chef's car when I needed to go to school. Life was good.

I loved that I was making my own money because, when the 4 siblings needed anything, I would use my credit card to buy them whatever they asked for.

When Rico found out about what I was doing, he didn't want me caring for my siblings alone. So, he would pay off my credit card from time to time; or he would give me money to purchase whatever was needed.

Rico was hard-working and came from a good background. He was working the side hustle that most neighborhood guys his age had. I was never a part of his side hustle, and he made sure nothing was happening around me.

Chef was a part of the after-school program at Englewood, and I would see her every day that I worked. We were still tight as ever too. I made her aware of Rico and my relationship and that I loved him. I told her what he did for work and about his side hustle.

She advised me to be careful and to stay focused in school. I listened and moved accordingly, swearing that I would never become a statistic by having babies and dropping out of school to be with a boy from around the way. Girls did that often where I'm from.

One day while at Chef's house, I introduced Chef to Rico over the telephone and then gave her the phone.

She said, "Hello. Nice to finally meet you!" She asked him, "Why do a side hustle instead of just working a regular job?

I was shocked like hell that she asked him about his side hustle, which I wasn't supposed to tell her or anybody about in the first place.

Rico, being silly and amusing, said something trying to be funny and break the awkwardness. But Chef didn't find him funny and gave me the phone back, and said, "If you want to be with something like that, go right ahead! That's your life that you'll be throwing away. I wouldn't be with a man like that."

Rico heard everything she said. And I was so scared. *She* was upset, and I didn't know what to do about what Rico heard her say.

Rico and I eventually got off the phone. Chef wasn't saying much as she took me home. It was clear that she did not like or want me with Rico because she actually told me herself.

"Good morning grandma." is what I remember saying when I walked into her room. She called my name each morning for me to help her as she was getting dressed for work. But this time was different.

When I came where she was and looked at her, my grandmother was slouched to the right with her clothes half on. I looked in her face and one eye was closed and her mouth was twisted. I tried to help her get dressed but her arm was heavy, and her words weren't clear.

I rushed to the back room and told Yolanda that grandma didn't look good.

Yolanda ran to my grandmother's room, and when she saw my grandmother, she screamed, "Call 911!!"

My grandmother had had a stroke. And I didn't know what to do. I was so afraid.

I went to the washroom, and I prayed, "God, heal my grandmother and do not let her die."

"This was a *massive* stroke." the Dr. said. "Your grandmother needs to go to rehabilitation before she can go home."

After coming home from School one day, Yolanda told me and my uncle that grandma wasn't coming back to the apartment we lived in and called home for the past 10 years.

Then we had to find somewhere to go by the end of the month. May-May and my niece Kierra had already moved out with her boyfriend/her daughter's father. By the end of the month, my uncle Cortez and I found a 2-bedroom apartment on 57th and Sangamon, not far from where we lived.

This street was one of the *busiest* in Chicago. It was a party block, the family block, and low-key, the get-money block. It wasn't Long before Cortez and Rico connected, allowing Rico to get keys to the apartment.

Oh No Not Me!

1999 is my college graduation year when I will receive my associate degree. I can't believe that I'm only months away from another stepping stone.

But of course, as my life has shown over and over again, there's always something that happens at a time like this; and *this* something is the most unexpected.

My worst fear is at my doorstep: I am pregnant.

I held this information for a couple of days before telling Rico. I didn't know what he would think of me now. Would he accept the baby? Is this what he wanted?

Finally, about a week had passed since I discovered I was pregnant. I remember telling Rico I was pregnant with his child. He replied, "Wow!" with a smirk on his face. But he soon realized that I was not smiling nor joyous about our situation.

He proceeded to ask, "What do you want to do?"

I said, "I don't know *what* I want. I don't believe in abortions."

"Neither do I." He responded immediately. And holding my hand, he said, "I'll support the baby if you want it. And if you don't (want the baby), I understood the pressure and I'll support you in the unknown as well."

It's Saturday morning a week later and I still haven't made a decision.

Rico and I are asleep in the bedroom when I awakened to knocks on the front door. Cortez answered and I heard familiar voices. It was my 4 younger siblings: Steve, Stephanie, Bonna and Nikki.

I remember opening my room door and feeling dirty and disgusting while watching my sister look at me half-dressed and in bed with a man. I did not like what I was showing my younger siblings.

And, the more I studied the bible, the more I felt as if I was doing something wrong. I was already uncomfortable with living together with Rico in sin. Even when we would be intimate, I would feel like I was going against what the Bible said about fornication.

I hurried to get dressed, then asked Stephanie, "How did y'all get to the house? And does Mrs. Allie Mae know you guys are here?

She said, "We took the bus to come find you. Also, me and Bonna need some shoes."

I looked down and saw that they definitely needed shoes. I got dressed and watched them go back home. On this very day, I realized that I couldn't set a good example for them while I was laying up with a man.

My mind started racing: "I have to finish school! I'm not married. I don't have the money to take care of my siblings *and* a baby! I cannot have this baby. My God! I have messed up *big* time. I'm going to be exactly what people said I'd be, that I would be no different."

Not that I thought I was better than anyone else, I just wanted to be better than what I was used to seeing around me. So, I started calling around looking for a clinic, and someone directed me to a clinic on the Eastside.

I decided to dissolve pregnancy, without telling Rico right away. I moved in with Chef to start over and for the accountability that I obviously needed.

I had not told my friends or family or Chef about the pregnancy.

I can already hear the words of Chef, and I could not take her words of judgment. I could not let her be right about me nor have her and her family angry with me, after all the work she has put in to make sure I did better in life.

But I *had* to tell Mrs. Johnson (B.J.) who was Dr. Kidd's assistant and friend; but also, someone I trusted and worked with in the night school program.

I begged her to swear to secrecy not to tell Dr. Kidd. And I had to tell her because I needed her to cover me when I left work to go get the abortion.

The day I went to get the abortion I was terrified. I didn't believe in abortions, but here I am…alone.

I'll never forget going into this gloomy, dinghy-looking clinic with this nonchalant nurse assisting me. She took the $225 payment, and she led me to a locker room to undress from the waist down. She told me to open the door when I was done, indicating that I was ready.

Going into the room where the abortion was to take place, there were gowns, swabs, and other objects everywhere.

As I came near to the stainless-steel table, still looking around, there was blood on the floor as well as bloody cloths and sheets in the corner of the room.

I asked the doctor, "Will I be asleep during the process?"

He said, "No, you will not be put to sleep, but it will be quick."

Everything in me knew I should get up and leave this place. Every sign there could possibly be to tell me that this place was not safe was right in my face.

Then the nurse tells me, "Lay back and place your feet in the handles at the bottom end of the table near the stirrups. The nurse raised my gown and covered my bottom half with a white sheet like the ones I saw on the floor.

She went to turn on a machine that housed a clear container that I could see underneath the towel that was used to cover it.

The doctor takes what looks like a suction wand by my thigh and some form of clamps and inserts this thing into my vagina. I immediately tensed up, and the nurse said to me, "Relax. A 14-year-old just left and didn't do all that you're doing."

"Well, I guess that's who's *blood* I see all over this place." I thought to myself.

The doctor moved the wand further into my vagina, and now I can feel and hear the suction. At this moment I screamed. I tried to be strong and hold it in, but I couldn't. I even had the nerve to cry while in my head I was asking God to help me!

I could literally feel everything the doctor was doing. I looked over my right shoulder and my view was the machine, which was the most horrific sight.

There was blood leaving from my body through a tube into the clear container that sat on the machine with the towel falling down from the machine which allowed me to see. I wept *so hard* while staring at this machine.

I said to the Doctor, "Stop."

The doctor ignored my first 2 requests, then he had the nurse come to the head of the table to comfort me. But her comfort was not received. Then, the nurse said, "The doctor *cannot* stop. He has to make sure everything is out."

My God! There was so much blood in this container. I just couldn't help but think this is not how this procedure should go!

After the doctor was done, the nurse helped me off the table and walked me into the locker room, instructed me to get dressed, and then I was free to go.

So, in excruciating pain, I managed to dress myself and drive myself back to Englewood.

CHAPTER 12

My perspective of myself was based on her view, and her view was toxic and controlling. She kept me from being exposed so that I wouldn't know better.

LPH

TRUST YOU, NOT THEY

LAKISHA P HUNTER

TRUST YOU, NOT THEY

I remember that, on May 20, 1999, I graduated from Lexington College with an associate degree.

My 2 years there were a struggle academically. I was able to get good grades, but I had to fight hard to make it. My past has caught up with me once again. There was so much I had to learn all over again.

RISE ABOVE THE ORDINARY: *The Life Behind Her Smile*

Many things were missed while I was in high school, and even grammar school. I didn't know a lot of fundamentals, like parts of speech, conjunctions, etc.

In writing, I didn't know the difference between too or to, rather and whether, and their and there.

I did not really accomplish learning these fundamentals until late adulthood. Even when going to pursue my bachelor's degree, I had to start at reading 100 and writing 101. I was now paying money for education that I could have gotten for free in grammar and high school.

I was busy being popular with the teachers in high school, banging in grammar school while passing to the next grade because of my age and using my learning disability as a crutch instead of taking advantage of all the learning opportunities placed before me.

Talk about your past catching up with you! I swore I would never be stupid again. I would learn on my own and I would never be stupid or uneducated about anything. I taught myself through trial and error, but I eventually learned the basics of reading and writing fundamentals.

At my graduation, my grandmother was there, and a very proud Dr Kidd and May-May were there with my niece, my daddy, Auntie Lillian and grandma too.

My father was so proud! I had a nice crowd of supporters. Chef and her husband were not there because they were out of town.

Following graduation, I was hired as a hostess on the dinner cruise boat on Navy Pier where I worked my way up to management for the next 12 years.

In the meantime, and in between times, Rico and I are seeing less of each other. Chef would allow him to come to visit me at her house, but he never came.

Whenever I *did* go out to see him back in the neighborhood when I would return, Chef would be silent or tell me how disappointed she was in my continuing to date Rico. She felt that I had too much going for myself to be dating him.

She said, "He's selfish and a street thug." But Rico was actually the total opposite.

She said, "How can you call yourself a Christian when you're having sex with a thug?!"

Rico realized that our conversation with each other was changing. He felt I always seemed irritated when talking to him while I was home. It was because Chef's comments were weighing in on me. I was exhausted from this situation with her and Rico.

I took into consideration that Chef was a Spiritual woman. She's a woman of wisdom and I respected her opinion.

He asked me, "What is the most important: what Chef thinks about me, or the love and respect I've shown you in the 2 years we've been dating? What we have built together in our relationship, or please her? She doesn't know how our relationship works. She knows nothing about us as a couple. That joke that she knew was only a joke, and it's not the reason she doesn't like me; she's using that as an excuse. It's always been about her controlling you."

I was in shock at his words because he never said a *thing* about Chef. If he had anything to say about her, he's never said it to me. He kept his opinion about her to himself all this time.

He continued, "Remember how I've supported you and how I've been here to push you in all of your endeavors? And how much I love you and how I've never disrespected or fussed with you? Or how we've never had an argument? Ever!"

I told him, "I don't know what to do. I owe her so much because she's done a lot for me. I don't want to disappoint her, and I don't want to lose you either."

He said, "She's controlling you, and I'm coming to get you! You're leaving with me. We will go find an apartment big enough for your sisters and brothers to come over and spend nights. I got you; I got us!"

I still didn't know what to do.

Shortly after hanging up the phone, the doorbell rang. It was Rico, coming to get me to take me away from Chef's house. But I couldn't leave like that.

Looking into his eyes, I could see that he was so hurt that I wouldn't come with him.

"Just you, me, and the kids!" he said.

But I couldn't hurt Chef like that. She's done so much for me, so I couldn't leave. And I remember crying for days for the pain I caused him.

God Will Help Me

Months have gone by and I'm learning more and more about the word of God.

I was very disciplined in the things of God. I studied every day. I supported pastor at speaking engagements, I was a part of the choir, and now I've been asked to be a deaconess.

"My goodness what an honor!" I thought.

Rico and I are still together, but Chef's words about Rico being bad for me flooded my mind because she feels he's not of God.

And now with my new church friends watching my moves, with anything I do I always wanted to do it right and want to make sure I was right and honest and true. So, I knew I had to have a conversation with Rico.

Standing on granny's porch one Sunday after church, Rico and I had a conversation about what our week looked like.

I told him, "I need to talk to you about your side hustle and our relationship. I don't think we need to be together anymore. I'm trying to better myself spiritually and be a good example for my siblings. But I can't continue this relationship with you if we aren't going in the same direction in God."

He replied, "I believe in God, and I was raised in the church. You are my soulmate and I love you."

"But we can't be together while you're doing your side hustle. It doesn't feel right. I can't support that." I told him.

He looked at me in my eyes and asked me, "Please do not break up with me. What I do on the side isn't more than you or our relationship, and I'm not willing to lose you over it. Be patient and let me handle this last thing that I have in front of me. And by the end of the week, I will be done with all of it. I promise."

We kissed and he said, "I promise you!"

I couldn't wait to tell everyone that Rico and I don't have to break up!

My friends were so happy! And granny and the rest of them were too, since they were listening by the window.

I made it home to talk about the news. But Chef didn't believe him saying, "If he really was going to do it, and if he really loved you as much as he claims he does, then he wouldn't need 'til the end of the week. He'd do it right now! But go-ahead, Mrs. I- believe-I'm-in-love. You'll see. He's not going to stop.

Now, I knew this wasn't the way the streets were made. You can't just leave situations like this instantly. It takes time.

But when the end of the week came, I heard nothing from Rico. I didn't call him throughout the week because I was fearful that he may change his mind, so I didn't want to jinx it.

I was so nervous! What guy would do what I asked him to do? I knew men always put their money first.

No word from Rico in *days*!

I thought, "I guess Chef was right: he chose the streets over me." I was *beyond* hurt.

Then one day I got mad and went to his house to express myself. But to my surprise, Rico's mother answered and told me that Rico got locked up a couple of days before. She said, "I don't have his information yet. But when I do, I'll make sure to give it to you."

I nearly fainted. My heart dropped to the bottom of my stomach. I know nothing about jail, and I didn't know what to do.

I had a ton of questions running in my head: "What happened? *How* did it happen? How will I see him? *When* can I see him? Where do I go?"

The bus ride home was the longest ever. I was a wreck! What was I going to do without him?

I didn't dare tell Chef about Rico being locked up right away. I didn't want to become disrespectful towards her, so I didn't say a word. I just went to my room and cried.

Shortly after that day, Chef wasn't saying much but was walking around humming songs and chipper like she knew something and was waiting for me to respond and admit to Rico being in jail. I'm not sure if one of my supposed *confidants* told her or not. But I believe she already knew.

When I was finally able to see and speak to Rico, he said, "I was arrested the very same day I was ending my connection with my side hustle! But I meant what I said. And I want to marry you. Will you marry me?"

About 2 months prior, sitting in the car in front of Rico's house, a song came on the radio - *"Ready Or Not"* by After 7.

This is the jam and we're both singing it. While singing, I hear Rico ask me, "Will you marry me?"

Not believing what I'd just heard, I asked him, "Repeat yourself please."

He asked again, this time with tears in his eyes, "I love you.

Will you, Lakisha Petrice Hunter, will you marry me?"

Without hesitation, I said, "Yes!"

With our song still playing in the background, we embraced each other with a kiss.

Trust What You See Not What They Say

In 2001, another change in my career took place. I was encouraged by Chef, and other culinary teachers I have come to know while working with Chef, to apply for a job with Chicago Public Schools as a Culinary teacher through ETC (Education To Careers) at Westinghouse High School where there was a position open.

I was 21 years old.

Needless to say, I did get the job; and so did another chef. That's how big this Culinary program was in this school.

I taught at Westinghouse for 5 years. During my time there, I could feel that the principal was not too fond of me. She felt I fed her false expectations in my performance.

Now, I may have agreed to give her all that she was looking for in the program, but I never signed up to be her "show-off" chef.

I would have *loved* to satisfy her expectations, but I had 130 students who were exactly like I was at age 15-18, except these were worse!

The Westside was completely different from the Southside. I noticed that the Westside schools had to fight hard for everything; whereas the Southside schools were spoiled because getting funding for what they needed came easier than for the Westside.

These students were actually living as adults. They were raising themselves, encouraging me to call their parents on them, and ensuring me their parents were not ruling over them.

When I did call some students home, the parents asked, "What do you want *me* to do about it?" Thus, proving the students' point.

Therefore, I had to change my way of talking when teaching and speaking to them. I spoke to them as the adults they showed me they were. I spoke their language, and in doing this, I gained their respect.

Due to the authority that I had in the position I held at my other job, I was able to hire some parents and students to earn some *honest* money; this kept them from being set out of the place where they lived.

Could Rico Be Right?

My job at Westinghouse ended after I was tricked by the principal and vice principal: The vice principal explained that some papers she was giving me was a good evaluation, said that I would get a copy of the evaluation, and had me sign the papers. But actually, I was signing myself out of a job.

The assistant principal and I were really cool with one another the entire 5 years I worked there; so, I trusted that she was being honest with me.

Yes, I signed something I had not read and that was my most learned lesson. However, I continued with my job at Navy Pier until I started working in the hotel management industry.

Before leaving Westinghouse, the relationship between me and Chef was stronger than ever at one point since Rico wasn't around. We talked more and more about everything; there were hardly any arguments, and we went everywhere together. We were mother and daughter for sure.

One of the members of the church, Ashley, was a professional in her career of nursing and she was also like family to me. To me, blood couldn't make us closer. She looked out for me when making important business decisions.

One day, I was approached by Ashley who was selling her house and moving into another house, and her house wasn't too far from Chef's house.

I had visited Ashley at her house a few times and I liked her house. She saw that I was doing good for myself - working 2 jobs, maintaining a solid income, and helping my siblings. She wanted to offer me her house before listing it on the market, and she also offered to help me understand everything.

As a gift for my accomplishments, she would price it for little of nothing. She also said, "I will help you pay the closing cost for the house if you can't afford it."

She wanted me to be able to get to a place where I could take in my siblings as I had always planned and shared with her. Then she began explaining how everything worked when buying a house.

Ashley came from a family of homeowners, so I trusted her and there was no reason for me not to. But it was scary and exciting at the same time. Buying a house is a big deal! But it felt right, and I was interested.

I shared the news with Chef and wanted her to talk with Ashley in case I missed anything in explaining it to her. Chef listened before offering her advice and opinion. When she finally spoke, she had a lot to say.

One thing I remember her saying is, "You're not ready for something so big, and there must be something wrong with the house because nobody is going to do all of that when they need money to move into wherever they're planning on moving. She must be rushing to sell her house to you so she can hurry and move into hers. But I guess she found herself a fool in you to want to do it."

"What makes me not ready? I thought to myself. I know nothing about the housing stuff, but this is not what Ashley explained to me. She did mention that she wanted to sell within a couple of months but wanted to check with me first and was willing to help however she can help me get the house.

I didn't know what to do but I felt Ashley was being honest.

But Chef told everyone in the house about the conversation and I heard some agreeing with her. She and I weren't seeing eye to eye on this, but I stayed silent.

After hearing her converse about the situation with everyone, she didn't say much to me for a couple of days; and I became depressed.

Now I'm thinking, "Was Rico right about her? Did she have control over me like he said she did?" Then I would dismiss it. "Nah, she just wants what's best for me." I said to myself.

So, I turned down Ashley's offer and continued living at Chef's house. Ashley listed the house, and it sold quickly. My heart was broken because I believed that that was my house.

New Twist New Love

Brian was a man who had a crush on me since high school. He was extremely persistent and never gave up trying to date me. He was a great friend too. He was comical and fun to be around.

Everyone knew Brian was crazy about me no matter who I was with.

Brian went away to college after high school. I hadn't seen him since. But he found out that I was living with Chef, so he reached out; again, *begging* me to be his woman and marry him.

I consistently responded, "NO! We are FRIENDS and FRIENDS ONLY. You keep asking me and we won't be FRIENDS anymore!"

Chef heard and knew Brian was pursuing me, but I wasn't interested in him any more than what we were, friends. She knew this even in high school and she too laughed at his pursuit. He was irritating me when it came to that. Brian was a church boy and silly, but he was my homie.

The next day there was a letter on my bed from Rico. He had written to me from jail. I still love him with all of my heart.

Later that day, Chef made her way to my room to ask a question for her understanding. She asked, "How can you love and want to be with a man in jail when there's a nice man like Brian who's about to graduate college, no kids, no drama, and is *crazy*-ready to marry you? Waiting for Rico is a big mistake when all he is going to do is go back to what he was doing before he went in, and you will have missed the best opportunity of your life. But it's your life. Throw it all away for a man who's not worth it."

Her energy about this situation ruled out Interactions with one another for days. I became lonely and missed Rico. I also became angry that he was locked up away from me and that I had to get used to life without him by my side.

I felt abandoned by him, unloved without him, and confused. In this state of emotions, Chef's last words weighed in on me. "Maybe she is right that I am stupid for writing and waiting. Maybe he should have stopped his hustle the same day I asked him to. But I'm tired of trying to defend our love to people! Maybe, just maybe he's not the one and Brian is."

I called Brian knowing he was going to ask me again to be with him, and this time I accepted his proposal.

Shortly after, I began looking for an apartment. I have been living with Chef for 4 years and thought it was about that time to grow up and move out into my own. I grew weary of the constant disagreements and the fact that I couldn't do anything right for myself.

I needed to get control of my life and I felt I couldn't do that while living with her.

I swear to God I'm appreciative of everything she has done for me! She's done more than my own family, and I am changed forever because of her. But I can't keep living like this.

When I found an apartment, I told Chef I was moving out. And she accused me of being sneaky and doing things underhanded.

Needless to say, when I left Chef's house, we were not on good terms. We hadn't spoken again for years!

That year during spring break, Brian came from college to properly propose. I accepted but, in my mind, I was thinking, "What the hell was I doing! I'm not in love with this man! I don't want to be married to him, but I could not hurt him in front of all the people. So, I said "Yes."

His mother and Chef were so happy, but I was so sad. "What was I going to do now?"

I begged God to get me out of this situation. "I don't want to be with him, nor Rico. I don't want to be with anybody! This is too much!" I cried out.

Months have passed and I'm still engaged. I finally accepted the fact that I got myself into this mess and I see no way out. Brian was the happiest man on earth about this engagement. Now I'm going to be married to someone I didn't love like that because I refuse to hurt him. After all he was my friend.

CHAPTER 13

Defeat becomes extinct once YOU make the decision for it to no longer exist in your life!
#ImWINNING.

LPH

LIFE'S MOST IMPORTANT SEEK

LIFE'S MOST IMPORTANT SEEK

I remember that it was the day before going to do wedding things with Brian. I was balled up on my living room floor under the cover feeling so sick and depressed until I was very weak.

I received a call from Brian saying, "I was just checking on my bride. And I want to talk to you about some news I just learned of. My ex-girlfriend at college is expecting my child."

I snapped in my head toward God: "Are you kidding me God??!!! Are you freaking kidding me??!!!!! Am I this bad of a person that I have to keep going through heartbreak after heartbreak? Is this what You do to those who follow You and are loyal to You? Why do You keep throwing people like this near me? Aren't You supposed to protect me from evil now that I'm following you?"

I'm 24 years old and have had more than my share of hurt in such a short time. I felt like I've been run over by a Mack truck.

Brian begged my forgiveness and wanted to still get married. However, I called off my marriage to Brian. And just like that I was free from marrying! Still, I was hurt and broken once again!

Be careful what you ask for because it just might be unbearable.

On the church front, my mom and stepdad broke up. My mom actually went back to my father after 16 years! They never divorced each other. They were married 28 years and separated for 26 of those years.

I didn't like them getting back together at all! My dad had been off drugs about 4 years now and I didn't want my mom to start him to using again.

I actually shared this with my dad when he told me they were back together. This is when my dad said, "Your mom isn't using drugs anymore, baby girl. Yea she drinks her beer, but she's doing *way* better with turning her life around."

I could not believe what I was hearing! My mom not using anymore is a blessing from God. My prayers have been answered!

I was a member of my church for 7 years at this point, and I love my pastor and his family. I loved *all* of my church family, and I was a committed member. I was *always* in church. I was very disciplined in my studying and in learning the things of God, I was a faithful tither, and I helped whoever needed anything.

However, many have taken advantage of my kindness; and sometimes I could see it. Although I was doing what

I did from my heart, I still didn't expect church people to be this way, nonetheless.

But this being my very first experience of this kind made me watch people more and learn behaviors of the real verses the fake.

I was a giver and stayed dressed to the nine.

I was making good money and bought any and everything I wanted: Gucci, red bottom heels, Armani, Dooney and Burk bags, Kenneth Cole shoes and clothes, Tahari suits, and Air Max gym shoes were my favorite gym shoes.

A Life Changing Experience

I went to a play called *If These H.I.P.S Could Talk* by David Tolbert; it was playing at the Regal Theater.

I invited a friend/co-worker from Westinghouse to go with me to see this play. She was raised catholic and was about 15 years older than me. I bought the tickets at the last minute on the same day as the play was playing. And some way somehow, we were seated in the first row of the theater. It was so amazing!

The play was so funny and very well acted. There was a scene that became very serious and relatable to most of the people attending the play.

I remember this scene having my full attention as if I were hypnotized.

I felt myself becoming vulnerable and sensitive shortly after an actress began singing a particular song. I'm not sure of the name of the song, but my hands lifted in worship and so did most of the audience.

At the end of the song, you could feel that the atmosphere shifted, and this was no longer a play; this was a worship center where the presence of God came in.

The singer/actress began worshipping and people were speaking in tongues. I had never heard anyone speak in tongues since I heard prophetess Juanita Bynum speak in tongues when she preached *No More Sheets*.

While watching Juanita Bynum teach on video, when I hear her speak in tongues on the video, I felt a leap in my belly that felt like a punch. I did not know what this was though.

I'm Called And Chosen

At the play, there's no music playing, just sounds of worship. People are speaking in tongues all over the place. But there was one distinctive utterance of tongues from what sounded like a man's voice that floated ever so lightly over everyone else to my ears. When I heard this sound, something came over me.

As I continued to hear the voice of this individual a second time, I began stuttering out of control until I was speaking in tongues, being filled with the holy ghost with the evidence of speaking in tongues!

My coworker, on the other hand, was stuck. She had no clue what was going on and was very concerned about me. She wasn't fearful but wasn't sure how I felt because I couldn't speak or explain at all as I drove her home.

But she knew that whatever happened to me was real and she was happy for what she knew added to my belief. She, from another belief, understood this better than those among whom I worship.

The next day I called my pastor for guidance on what took place the day before. I asked, "What are these tongues that I'm speaking? What does this mean? What happens next? I need instructions."

My pastor directed me to the Bible: 1 Corinthians 14: 27- *[27] If any man speak in an unknown tongue, let it be by two, or at the most by three, and that by course; and let one interpret. [28] But if there be no interpreter, let him keep silence in the church; and let him speak to himself, and to God.*

My pastor explained that, basically, this scripture passage was letting me know that I should only speak in tongues in private; not in church nor any open place, but only in private prayer time in my home with God.

"But why did it come and why was I filled in the open if it's to be private?" I was thinking.

But of course, my pastor knows more than I. I trust and believe he is led by God as far as I knew that to mean.

After that encounter, I was not the same person. It felt as if I was missing something Spiritually and I needed to find out what it was. There's so much I don't know and so much I'm hungry for in the things of God.

I could see and feel my search become more diligent, which led me to begin visiting other churches. I have to see what God is mapping. But I was a committed and loyal member of my church home.

In the next year, God had shown me vision after vision of me preaching the word of God. I would be wide awake and driving sometimes when God would give me this vision.

Now, this was *never* a desire of mine. All I wanted and prayed for often was to have a closer relationship with God and to help people who were less fortunate than me.

I gave to people on an everyday basis: No one could be around and in need and I do not help. Those I knew personally and even strangers I would give my last to. Showing care, love and concern towards other filled voids in my life.

When it came to friends, family, and church family especially, they could ask anything of me; whether it be out of my way or causes a stretch in my resources, I made it happen. This is how I'm made up. God has been good to me so in return I was good to people.

As much as I wanted to speak again, I never spoke in tongues again while under my pastor's leadership.

I began conversing with God for understanding, "God, what did this mean? I don't have the intelligence or the know-how to do what you're asking me to do. No one is going to want to listen to me, God. You *know* I had an abortion, right? I'm still struggling with that, mentally. I'm still dealing with the visions I have from when I was in the clinic and laying on the table and seeing the machine. Lord, I even hear the suction. I can't even bring myself into repentance because I'm so ashamed of what I've done. I feel dirty and unworthy. I don't deserve Your forgiveness; I can't even forgive myself!"

It was years before I was actually able to bring myself to a repented state of mind and loosed from the guilt of having an abortion.

"I'm dealing with more than enough, and now this? I'm going to be a laughingstock if I tell people I'm supposed to preach. People don't believe in women preachers. I don't even know if *I* believe in women preachers!" This was all in my head.

Even with me mentioning all of this, God still gave me visits, and now *dreams*, of me preaching the gospel…even me standing on a larger-than-large platform laying hands on thousands.

"Clearly, this is my subconscious revisiting something I've seen on TV! This is *not* being interpreted correctly." This was my rationale of what was happening with me.

Not You Too Brutus

Eventually, I went to my pastor to share with him what I've been going through. I told him, "I'm afraid to sleep because I don't want to dream dreams of me preaching! I believe God is telling me that I am called into the ministry. Is that what all of this means?"

My pastor was so elated to hear this news! He said, "I've been asking God in prayer to show me if the church is growing in the way He would have it to grow."

And he believed I was the sign that God decided to send to my pastor to give him his answer.

He said, "I want you to stand before the church and announce your being called into the ministry."

I immediately and directly said, "No! I'm not ready! I just wanted to share with you and receive directions on how to handle what I'm going through. I don't believe this is the direction I'm ready for. So, I'd rather wait."

He assured me and said, "The time is now. You've been very diligent, devoted, and faithful to the ministry."

When Sunday came, I did as my pastor asked me to: I stood before the church and announced that I have a call on my life to minister the word of God. I wept the entire time while I was making the announcement.

I mean, I was so jacked up and crying so hard until the congregation was not able to make out or understand what I was saying. So, my pastor and others repeated what I said.

And my pastor then said, "And I stand in agreement with what God is doing in her at such a young age. Her trial sermon will be announced soon! Now, y'all encourage her at the end of service."

So many members of the church were so excited about this announcement and told me so!

I, on the other hand, felt so convicted over all the things I had done: the people I fought, fornication, using profanity, being dishonest, having an abortion, drinking, smoking, and this list can go on.

"I am not worthy to be chosen to such a sacred assignment! Do these people know where I come from? Does God remember who my parents are? My family's generational struggles? The history of my family?" are just *some* of the thoughts that were going through my head.

My trial Sermon date was set for September 3rd. And I invited everyone I knew from grammar school, high school, and college. There were so many people coming to support and witness Englewood's Success Story go up another level.

Sept 3rd is here, and I attended the regular afternoon service. The special service for my trial sermon was scheduled for 3:30pm.

I was sitting in the choir stand where I normally sit, and my pastor began to give reflections on the church announcements just before offering the altar call.

There was something that my pastor mentioned in his reflections, but I had no idea what was shared because I was talking to the person sitting next to me. But, when I looked up, everyone was looking at me with concerned faces.

However, I went down before the altar to get prayer for the 3:30pm service along with others who came for prayer; but, for some reason, everyone was still looking at me with the same concerned look on their faces.

I walked over to Courtney's aunt and close friend of mine and asked her, "What was said earlier that has everyone in awe or concerned?"

She replied, "He said there will not be a 3:30pm Service today. But isn't that the service when you're supposed to preach?"

I didn't respond. I just walked away and went back to the alter call line.

I looked up at my pastor who was praying from the pulpit and realized he avoided looking in my direction.

Now, my pastor never told me that he was canceling the service, so I did not know what was going on. We hadn't had a conversation prior to that Sunday that would make me believe or aware there wouldn't be a service.

So, all I knew to do at this point was to leave out the side door.

Granny's grandson Derrick, who also had become my best friend, followed me. I didn't have my car and I wanted to get out of sight before everyone else came out to ask questions or see if I was ok.

Derrick asked me, "What do you want to do or where do you want me to take you? The only safe place I could think of was Bonita's mom's house – we called her "Madea."

Derrick and Bonita are members of the church who adopted me as their goddaughter; Bonita is also Granny Robert's daughter-in-law.

Madea and I are closer than blood relatives. I sought the advice of her and Bonita often. I loved my heart-to-heart conversations with them.

Once I arrived at Madea's house, she was dressing and getting ready for the 3:30pm service. She never noticed the look on my face until she noticed the silence between Derrick and I.

She turned her head towards us swiftly as she sat down at the dining room table and asked us, "What is wrong?"

All I could do was weep on her lap.

Derrick explained the situation to Madea and went back to the church to inform my guests that the service was canceled.

Here I am trusting people and again being hurt by people who I thought I could trust: My Pastor / Spiritual Father.

And to this very day, I *still* don't know why he canceled my service. Since then, I tried meeting with him, but he was never available to meet.

The Spirit Commands Growth

In March of that very next year while sitting in the choir stand, something came over me which I believe I can describe as scales falling from my eyes causing me to see clearly. It was like I had come to myself: I did not see me growing in my church home. I now saw that I have come as far as I was going to come in my home church; to the point that it was time to leave my home church.

I heard in the Spirit, "This will be your last Sunday here." I then repeated what I heard to my godmother and godfather who sat in the pulpit.

Concluding what the Spirit was saying, I realized I had been a faithful member for the past 7 years. With this understanding, I felt so relieved and at peace.

I had no plans on leaving my church before coming to service on this day. I loved every member and some I considered my family, and even to this day. But even Jesus had a "Judas" amongst Him.

Zion Temple gave me my foundation and I do not regret becoming a member, nor my experience there.

In all, I'm grateful to God for bringing me to Zion Temple where I brought so many to Christ: my siblings, cousins, old friends, and my aunts had joined Zion Temple as well; all through me bringing and inviting them to worship with me.

They saw firsthand my transformation, and how I was committed to the pastor, the church, and building the Kingdom of God through bringing people to Christ. There's more that I needed in God, and I know finally that I wasn't going to get it here.

However, Pastor Davis (my pastor) refused to meet with me so I could let him know of my decision to leave. Therefore, I wrote in a letter that I will no longer be a member and why. I gave the letter to both of my ministry's leaders, the leader of the deaconesses, and the leader of the choir.

Since I reverenced all of these leaders as *my* leaders, I would not just "jump ship" (leave the church) without letting them know why.

I did not want to talk with anyone else about my decision to leave the church. I also gave the same letter to my pastor's secretary to give to him; that way I was certain he would receive my letter.

In all honesty and in total innocence, I had no idea this would cause so much ruckus.

By the time Sunday came, everyone in the church heard about my letter, which wasn't a big deal to me. It was a well-written letter that explained my reason for leaving; and expressed that I had no idea what I had done to be treated like an outcast by my pastor.

How I've tried calling, pretty much begging, to meet, but to no avail.

I was hurt but I was not leaving in anger. I truly wished the church well.

It was later brought to my understanding that it was said that Pastor ordered the deacons to put me out of the church if I ever came to service. I was no longer welcome at the place that once felt like home.

There was a church I was very fond of which was not far from my former church; actually, the pastor of this new church used to be a member of Zion Temple. I know the young pastor through my godparents who would visit the church; and I would sometimes tag along.

By the summertime, I still was without a church home, but I was still with God.

One weekday I went to visit this new church that I had in my mind without my godparents. But on this particular day, they were having an outdoor tent service, and it was raining so hard and so badly until the deacons and members were pushing the water with push brooms from under the tent.

Yet, ministers were praying on microphones and the entire neighborhood could hear. They were actually praying for the rain to stop: "God, we pray that You hold back the rain that we may move forward with what You have called us to do so that the lost souls may come in the tent asking, 'What I must do to be saved?'"

I remember thinking in my head while looking around at everyone else praying, "Oh Lord, these people are crazy! How the world do they think the rain is going to stop just because they prayed for it?" While laughing, I said, "I'm getting the *hell* out of here!"

The woman praying on the mic was Minister Lisa. The harder it rained, the harder she prayed it seemed like.

As I stood to leave the tent, Minister Lisa let out a very strong and loud wailing sound called travailing. Then she spoke in tongues like I heard at the play a year ago; and how I sounded when I spoke but hadn't spoken since. It was the most anointed and amazing, authoritative sound I have ever heard!

And suddenly, guess what happened: the rain ceased, and the sun came out!

Now it could have been a coincidence that the rain stopped suddenly; maybe it could have been in the weather report for it to stop raining at that exact time.

But whatever the case may be, this got my attention, and I sat back down in my seat and checked my faith.

What's most important is I learned that day to never doubt what God can do when we pray in faith and believe that it can be done.

After that day, I visited the tent service every night that week. I'm thinking, "This may be the church for me." I never considered joining this church before because it was often said that women came to this church because the pastor was handsome and single.

It was also said that all the young girls wanted the pastor, and I didn't want to be categorized with that kind of women and rumors.

The Pastor was not my reason for wanting to join. What they have in this church is something I know nothing about; outside of the bible, that is: The Holy Spirit with the evidence of speaking in tongues.

They are openly speaking in tongues. They are not in secret speaking in their tongues. So, why did Pastor Davis say I had to speak in tongues in secret? I was so confused about that now. But I'm thinking this is the place where I can become un-confused.

The power and energy in this church was pulling me in like a rope around my waist. Some nights I couldn't sleep for thinking about this church.

I truly thought I would be at Zion Temple for the rest of my life. But visiting this church made me feel like I had been in the dark for the past 7 years; as if there's a whole world out here and I'm just now finding it. And, most importantly, this church is speaking my language and speaking to my spirit.

Finally, after weeks of contemplating, I joined the church. I was scared out of my mind, but I joined. That morning, I joined what would now be my *second* church.

My goodness, I don't like the sound of that! I have always believed that a church home is supposed to be that forever home until God calls you home.

On that morning, I attended Sunday School and joined in the afternoon service. As I walked to the altar, I was praying, "Lord, please let this be *Your* will. I pray this is the right church for me." The Lord gave me a sign that this is the place for me, but I'm *so* scared.

As I'm walking and praying, the tears are flowing down my face. At the altar, the Pastor hugged me. As I mentioned earlier, the pastor knew who I was through my godparents, whom he was *very* close to as a godson of theirs as well.

I remember the pastor was so happy that I joined, along with the 3 others. He instructed the altar workers / prayer warriors to take us to the back room to continue praying for us.

I'm still crying and the young lady who prayed for me said, "God told me to tell you that He has called you here today and this is your church. God said you have made the right decision. You can trust this pastor. God said do not be afraid."

Then she began praying that I would receive the Holy Spirit with the evidence of speaking in tongues. Seconds later, I began speaking in tongues. I couldn't believe that every question, thought, and prayer that I had in my head when joining, through this young lady God answered.

The person who prayed for me was a praise team singer - Paula Dickens. And we have been best friends since that day... 20yrs!

CHAPTER 14

Be wise in your decisions, be patient in your steps, be mindful of those you offend and empathetic to those who offend you.

LPH

HOME SWEET PFOM HOME

HOME SWEET PFOM HOME

I remember when I become a proud, gracious member of Prayer and Faith Outreach Ministries. What I have been experiencing in God's word is so refreshing. I know when experiencing something new people are always excited. But this joy that I have, the world didn't give it to me; and I didn't have it before joining PFOM.

Since joining, I'm not so serious all of the time. My feet felt lighter, my attitude was much sweeter, and I found my sense of humor at this church. I can be funny, I can laugh, and I can be myself, and still be saved.

New Church And Growing

Archbishop William Hudson III, who was presbyter at the time, is the name of my Pastor; and yes, he is single. But all I'm interested in *still* is the Word of God that he teaches.

This was the first church I've been in where there's no huge picture hanging on the wall of the pastor, or of those who came before him.

Come to find out he was the founder of this church, since he was just 17 years old, and has been preaching since he was 8 years old.

He was ordained at 12 years old. His father nor his mother were preachers.

Speaking of his family, this was also the first time I've seen a pastor's family act as regular members. They are so cool and down to earth. and relatable - like Archbishop Hudson.

There were no special seats or "parking reserved" signs for the family. His mother (Mom Hudson) and Sister (Tina) helped get the service ready, sang in the choir, served food in the kitchen, cleaned the washrooms, and whatever else was needed.

They are also such giving people. Archbishop's dad (Daddy Hudson) was a businessman but was also there to support, protect, and offer business and street advice if needed. He was full of knowledge about anything and everything.

This is all new to me. I know I've only been saved for a short 7 years, but I've been to many churches in the 7 years traveling with my former pastor to speaking engagements and just visiting other churches on my own or with my godfather Derrick. Searching for what I was missing at Zion Temple

I finally worked up the nerve to schedule a meeting with my new pastor to have a discussion with him about some of the questions I had about some of the things I've experienced with speaking in tongues and visions and dreams of me preaching. He shared with me what speaking tongues meant and that he sees that there's ministry in me, but I need to start as a deacon first.

I didn't come to this church to preach at all, and I was so glad that he could see ministry in me (to me this meant I didn't make this up; that I really did hear from God). But I did turn down becoming a deacon. I was just a deacon at Zion Temple for almost 4 years. I'm good at that.

He went on to explain that he would like to make me a deacon in training because he knew I was a deaconess at Zion Temple, and because of the ministry he sees in me, but I need to be trained and taught how to be a servant in the Lord's house.

He was such a wise person at such a young age! This is what I wish my former Pastor would have said to me and just taught me what all of this meant.

I told the Archbishop I would consider it.

Archbishop then asked, "How are you doing since you left Zion Temple? Did you do things in order before you left?"

I told him what happened with my trial sermon situation, and that, while deciding to leave, I wrote a letter letting Pastor Davis know that I was leaving and why.

He explained, "Ok. I just asked because it is important that you left in the right way. If you had not, I would have to pause your membership until you did things in order with your former pastor."

Archbishop accepted the fact that I gave a letter to my former pastor explaining the reason for me leaving as me leaving in an orderly fashion.

I am currently in my 21st year of being a member of now The Powerhouse Chicago (formally known as Prayer and Faith Outreach Ministries [PFOM]).

In Other News

In 2003, right before joining PFOM, I started spending a lot of time with my family on my dad's side.

Before I started going to church, my grandma Burneda's Godsisters (known to me as my Aunt B and Aunt Eunice), would often call them about my behavior in school and being arrested.

I so loved my aunts, and I loved being around them. My Aunt Eunice was the Assistant Pastor of her Church at McKenzie Missions. My Aunt Eunice stayed on her knees praying for me!

And now that I am changed and into the things of God, my grandma is still calling my Aunt; except now she's complaining that I'm in church too much! Grandma says, "She's too young to be so serious! She don't have *any* kids, and she has a *good* job. She needs to be traveling the world!"

One day, I'm on my way to my cousin Bertha's house (Aunt B's daughter) for a party with my cousin Tanisha - we were very close and both of us were raised by our grandmothers.

There were so many people there for the party! Family came from all over, old friends from around the house, and there were people I hadn't seen in *years*; even *one* person in particular. It was like looking at a ghost!

I couldn't *believe* what I was seeing, of who was staring back at me from afar. We just stared for a few moments with our mouths open; then eventually walked towards one another.

I thought this man was dead! But he's obviously not.

It was Damone…My Clyde. We hugged and basically screamed each other's names. We looked at each other and hugged again, not believing that we hadn't seen each other in 10 years.

We caught up on old times for *months* after the party. He was fine! I mean this man was a *man's* man! He walked, talked, and *smelled* like a real man. He was so strong until I felt so safe whenever I was around him.

We were friends for about a year before we decided to start a relationship. He was an A student of the Bible, as well as a teacher of the Bible, at his church. I loved learning from him.

We dated for almost 2 years, but it was as if we were in a long-distance relationship. I was working 2 jobs while going to school to obtain my B.A. in food and beverage management at Roosevelt University. He was in school as well. But when we did see each other, it was *fireworks*.

I *loved* my friend. We were great friends more than anything else. It wasn't the same love that I found with Rico, but it was a love that I cherished, even until this very day.

After a while something came to me that I remembered from my past with Damone: his behavior changed when he was with other girls.

I was young back then, but I always felt in my gut when something wasn't right. Even now, we aren't together or around each other a lot. I was traveling with friends to Miami, Atlanta, and often without mentioning it to him until I was already gone as if I wasn't in a relationship.

But the even stranger part is that he didn't give me any attitude about it, which grabbed my attention.

By the end of the Summer of 2005, history had repeated itself. I found out that Damone had another woman pregnant. And you could have bought me for a penny!

I didn't walk away in silence this time; I confronted the situation. He lied, but I knew it was true; therefore, I ended the relationship.

I was hurt about that situation, but it didn't really shake my foundation because I knew who he was.

Damone and I, after a while, continued being friends, but we weren't as close as before for a while.

It is often said, "A leopard never changes its spots." So, believe what you see, not what they tell you.

Church was going well and so was my job. I helped open a bookstore at the church, and I was cooking and making new friends. I just love people, but I'm very watchful. I joined the Mime Ministry and the young people looked up to me.

So far, I have learned a lot about gifts and callings, prayer and intercession, fasting, the Holy Spirit, and servanthood. Church is exciting, the people are excited, and I was at church all of the time because it was my safe space.

"I need to stay close to the saints of God who are focused on doing the things of God." was my thoughts. This helped me stay out of trouble.

I still hadn't talked to Chef in years. But she kept tabs on me through my sister Stephanie, who was also a student of hers.

I was doing good in my training as a deacon. And I'm growing more and more spiritually.

Oh No Not Daddy

In Sept 2004 in the afternoon, I was called off my job for an emergency with my father: His lungs collapsed because the HIV was hitting his body hard.

After all this time of working hard to become and stay clean from drugs, why does he have to endure this?!

My father had remarried, but not to the mother of his 3 young children ages 3, 5, and 9, whom he had custody of. And now, things weren't looking so good for my father. The doctor didn't think my father was going to make it through the night. There was no one to get the kids at the time, so I had to get them and bring them home with me.

I'm thinking, "I *gotta* be dreaming!"

My father was in a medically induced coma, by the doctor's orders, to give his body a chance to fight while they performed a surgery that put a balloon around his lung to keep him from dying.

My dad's coworkers and my coworkers came to the hospital in support. Some of them couldn't take seeing my dad lying in the hospital like that because it was very bad.

It was touch and go the first night and they were there supporting me through it.

The doctor told me the next couple of days will be critical. He said, "Now, it's up to him to live. We've done all we could do."

By the time my grandmother got there, she was worried and concerned about my dad. I gave her all the information that had been given to me. But she wanted to talk with the doctors herself. When the doctors came to talk to the entire family, my father's wife didn't want to come to the hospital or be involved in any way. She was so afraid of him dying.

The doctors told my grandmother that I chose not to sign the DNR (Do Not Resuscitate) form when they explained to me what that meant. Why did Grandmother interrupt the doctor and ask, "Why were you talking to her? *I* am his mother."

The doctor explained, "Since his wife was not around, she was the next of kin. So, she was the only one who could make decisions."

Before I could say anything, my grandmother snapped on me, saying, "You think you grown! You don't make no *damn* decision for my son! You think you better than everyone! You gone regret this very night!"

Angrily I replied, "No, I don't want to! Let my grandmother be in charge, Doctor. She's his mother. I don't want it!"

The Doctor said, "You could, but papers need to be filled out."

By this time, my grandmother had left the hospital cursing and crying.

My grandmother was a strong, independent woman who worked hard for us to have what we sometimes didn't appreciate. She never missed work. Her knees were so bad that she had to scoot down the stairs to make it to the bus stop at 5:30am every morning, having to take 3 buses to take care of others as a homemaker.

She'd come home and have to crawl up the stairs some days because of the amount of pain she was in.

She never stopped and never gave excuses. She did what she was supposed to do as a single mother: Fight.

I am the mother that I am today because of her drive and her strength for family.

I've learned that the lashing out that she often did was due to the situations and circumstances life brought her; and sometimes it was displayed negatively, which caused her to react in the ugliest and most hurtful ways.

She learned how to be a mother on her own, even though she had a story. But with our elders, there's no transparency. They don't share things of their past to help the younger generations to relate and understand. It's just "do as I say" without explanation.

Now that I'm older, I get it...I truly do. I know in my heart she wanted better for me; better than the life and experiences life threw at her.

Time Brings About Change

It's time for the school year to start. I need to get my sisters and brothers into school. They needed clothes and school supplies and Auntie Yolanda made sure they had all of the above.

My father was still in the hospital for 2 of the longest months of my life. He missed his kids, and his kids missed him. It was a slow process before things got back to normal for my dad, but he is alive.

My grandmother hadn't talked to me for a while now after that day at the hospital.

June 10, 2006, I have been working on the boat still, and it's now been years.

Damone called me out of the blue while I was working to see what I was doing. He decided to meet me downtown one summer night, and we walked and talked the night away, catching up and talking about our individual futures.

It was such a beautiful night to stroll the beachfront. And, no matter what, I always felt protected around him; so, I didn't have any fear of anyone bothering us.

We got tired of walking and decided to sit on the beach to continue our talk. By now, it's late and it's time for me to get home.

Neither one of us wanted the night to end. And…on this very night, I conceived a child with Damone.

When I realized I was pregnant, things were calm in my life: my siblings were older, and my life was steady. But I was still scared.

See, I wasn't where I wanted to be in life. While Damone was happy about the pregnancy, I had mixed feelings at the time. I was thinking, "Am I ready for a baby? I'm 27 and just finished taking care of kids."

Fear came all over me, especially when it finally hit me that I was still in training to be a leader in my church. "Oh Lord! The same thing is happening again! I *can't* let the youth down. I am so embarrassed, people are going to shame me, and I'll be the talk of the church. I've been celibate for 3 years and the one time I have sex I'm pregnant! Kisha, why are you so darn fertile?" I was thinking to myself.

"Nah! I'm *not* having this baby!" And my mind was made up as if I had forgotten about the devastation of the 1st abortion.

While setting up for the yearly tent service for our church, I'm thinking, "I have to get this abortion as quickly as possible before I start showing! I'm already 2 months."

I was setting up the bookstore outside. While I was setting up, my attention turned to a blank wall of a building that I was standing next to.

Out of nowhere, everything was silent. I heard no cars or people talking…just silence, as if I went deaf.

Then I heard a loud, weighty voice say to me, "If you do this, you will not get up from it."

I was stuck and in shock.

I knew I heard what I heard, but there was no one else around. But somehow, I knew the voice that was speaking to me. The audible voice of God came again seconds after the first, saying "If you do this, you will surely die." Then I heard no more.

I was in awe of what just happened. I ran and got in my car and cried so hard.

I told a trusted friend, Lamekia, about the pregnancy, and she didn't tell anyone.

"I know what God said, but this is crazy!" I thought.

And to make sure I didn't go through with the abortion, I had to tell Paula. I texted Paula a message telling her, "I'm pregnant." I can see her from where I was standing in the back of the tent.

At the end of service, she came to me with an authoritative voice, "You're keeping this baby. You will not be embarrassed or ashamed. Forget what you think anyone has to say about it. And, if anyone says anything out of the way to you about it, send them to me and I'll handle it from there." Once again, she was addressing the very thoughts and conversations I had with God.

It felt good knowing so many people in the church had my back and didn't shame me. This was new territory.

I told my pastor, but he didn't believe me at first. I called him from work and said, "I am pregnant."

He responded, "Pregnant with what? A new anointing?"

I laughed so hard. Now, I understand that my pastor has my back, so I wasn't fearful anymore.

Archbishop had to sit me down from leadership and had me talk with the youth, apologizing if I caused any confusion in their walk with Christ by my actions.

He also encouraged me throughout my pregnancy.

He explained to me, "Your *actions* were a sin, but your baby is a blessing from God. Do not be fearful. Know that God knew this would happen. You are still who God called you to be, you just slipped up. Repent and seek God while moving forward."

6 months later on a Sunday, Archbishop Hudson spoke words of encouragement over my life and my baby before the whole church.

He said, "God said that, because of your obedience to what I told you, you will not have a painful pregnancy or delivery. Your child will want for nothing as long as he lives." His voice trembled as if he was about to cry as he repeated it again, "God said, you obeyed my voice and now I will reward you."

I never told him about my encounter with God that day. But God was showing him now.

CHAPTER 15

The Moral of the story *The Life Behind Her Smile* is.... It's Genuine!

It's not about me: "My experience was formed to help someone reading this book."

LPH

AND IN MY CLOSING

AND IN MY CLOSING

I remember that, after deciding to keep my baby, Damone was happy. But he also understood the hesitation that I had.

He knew who I was to the youth around me and how my walk with God was everything to me. So, he felt obligated to ask me to marry him to keep me from the embarrassment we both thought would come from the church.

I declined his proposal since I understood why he proposed. But I will always love him for asking and the reason he did.

Damone and I remained friends; best of friends at that. I thank God that Archbishop Hudson didn't shun me, or I would have married in fear of how the church would respond, although I wasn't looking to be married.

I had a great support team within my church, and I was truly blessed as God said he would do, but I'm still afraid of people's reactions - those of my past and those from my former church.

Revelation Joy For Warfare

On March 9, 2007, I gave birth to my son - Christian Isaiah Hunter, my love child. My dad, Paula, Lamekia, Anita, Em Dee, and my baby sister Verlene were all in the delivery room with me. Yes, all 6 there!

I was afraid and I needed my community with me. But the labor and delivery were not that painful, as God promised it would not be.

Birthing him taught me a love that's indescribable but obtainable. I never knew love like this before and I made sure I gave him the words "I love you" and not just my actions. I wanted him to hear his mother *say,* "I love you."

I wasn't going to have a baby shower but two good sister-friends from church, Simone and Anita, talked me into it. At My baby shower, I had so many gifts until they filled 2 bedrooms in my apartment. So much so that I didn't have to buy anything for my son for almost 2 years! Gifts came well after the shower too.

But you *know* with all this *joy* that I have now, the enemy had to stick up his ugly head!

Shortly after my baby was born, my grandmother died.

I lived right next door to the senior citizen building where she lived. I could not believe she left us. But I'm so glad she and I were able to reconcile this past year and that she was able to hold her great-grandson who she thought was the most handsome little baby.

Regardless of everything negative my grandmother said in my life, all that she instilled in me I will always cherish. Life made her bitter at times, but I loved and do love her dearly and never held any of the hurtful things she said to me.

But in my grandmother's passing, Yolanda and I grew closer.

They say grandchildren give grandparents a do-over and they get to get it right the second time around. Well, my mom did just that.

She was drug-free and remarried. I love the supportive grandmother and mother she was to me and for me. Christian was her 5th grandchild, and they all loved their grandma Rochelle.

She had a soft spot for them as well.

Kids had always liked being around my mother because she was always a fun person. My Aunt Lillian's kids were like my mother's own children.

We talked a lot about the past during the 2 years she babysat for me while I worked. She accepted responsibility in her own way, and she never denied any of the situations that took place - she owned it all.

Many ask if I ever resented my mother for the way I was brought up and her abandoning me and my siblings.

I remember, years before having Chris, that I called my mom to curse her out about the things of the past.

She asked, "Why are you asking? Why and where is this coming from? We talked about this."

But, interrupting her, I kept going with what I had to say. And when I went to use my choice of curse words, I started stuttering. Without any control of my own, I started stuttering every time I tried to curse her. Then my mouth became muzzled.

God literally muzzled my mouth to the point that I couldn't say anything until after I hung up the phone.

Once I hung up the phone, the Holy Spirit brought the scripture to my mind, "Thou shall honor thy mother and father." And, another scripture came to mind, Proverbs 28:21 "Life and death is in the power of the tongue: and those who love it will eat the fruits of it."

God did not allow me to be disrespectful to my mother, and it was not in my heart to do so. I was only expressing feelings that others thought I should feel.

I had allowed someone close to me to convince me somehow that I was angry and needed to release this anger from my mother.

After that phone call, I felt silly and ashamed.

I have never disrespected my mother, and I never even thought to. Some way somehow, I never passed fault or blame to my mother.

Yes, I had every right to; but I don't recall even thinking about how I felt towards my mom concerning my upbringing, not to the point where it would bring me to the place and point of disrespecting her.

So, I repented like I've never repented before! And I apologized to my mother days later.

Oh Happy Day Indeed

In 2016, my mother joined the church where the rest of my siblings and I worshiped.

On September 3rd, my father received the worst news of his life.

I took him to the hospital because he wasn't feeling well. It was on this day that doctors came into the room and told my dad, his new wife (his last wife died of cancer), and me that my father didn't have long to live, and that he will probably pass away any day now.

I was by his side the entire time. I didn't know what to do or how to feel. I was numb and couldn't feel a thing.

After that day, I kept busy by doing everything for my father and my youngest siblings. I had to because I couldn't take another hit like this.

"God, this is my father…. MY FATHER!! There's no way You are taking him away from us like this. He's too young: he's only 54 years old! He's supposed to have more time than this. First, my Aunt Nikki died before the age of 40 from pneumonia. My grandmother is gone at 64. And now my dad?

I am literally *Yelling at God* in the hospital chapel!

After calming down, I wept as I sat on the bench… remembering that 5 years ago doctors counted him out, *but* God didn't. Instead, God brought him back to us and gave us 5 more years of life. "Father God, I repent for what I just said to you…………"

I drifted into some of the memories of my father and me together. We had a love for old-school music. Everyone in our family knew this. We'd compete with our CD collection, but he had me beat.

He had everybody's soul CD that existed. He had a total of 911 CDs. One day at a BBQ, his wife's cousin asked to have a CD. He told her, "No! This is *sacred* between me and my daughter; and if anything was to ever happen to me, she would get all of my music and equipment!"

But after receiving this news, my dad said, "Let's go to the movies." So, that's what we did.

We picked up the other kids and went to see *Columbiana*. But his wife stayed behind.

I remember looking at my dad wondering, "What is going on in his head? What was he thinking?"

I really had to fight back the tears to keep the kids from asking questions. And I didn't want my father concerned.

After leaving the movies, I asked my father, "Are you scared?"

He said "Yes, I am. But I can't change it. So, I have to accept it."

At that moment, I didn't see what my father felt (scared). I saw the strength of my father…strength like no other.

I love him and admire him even the more because he took dying like a real O.G.!

My father's wife was jealous of my relationship with my father and her actions showed it. Therefore, I didn't care for her too much either.

I shared the doctor's news with the rest of my family and friends, and people came from all over to see my dad. But his wife wouldn't allow anyone into the house to see him. My father was aware that people were coming to visit him, but his wife said "No." She would not allow even his own kids to visit him. She tried to keep them from coming into their bedroom to see him.

One morning, my little sister called to tell me what my father's wife was doing. I rushed over to see what the issue was; and to his wife's surprise, I was at their house bright and early in the morning.

She opened the door, and my little brother ran inside. She tried to stop him, but he pushed her down.

My father saw everything and started yelling at her saying, "Stop trying to keep my family from seeing me!"

But she wouldn't listen.

So, my father told me, "Help me get dressed and take me home with you."

"Gladly!" I responded.

When I got him to my house, I prepared a bath for him. After helping him to the washroom, I closed the door, went into my room, and prayed to God for strength.

My father was a saved man who believed in Jesus Christ and was also a member of my church. He loved and protected Archbishop Hudson.

I was able to take my father to church on that Sunday and Archbishop was preaching a message entitled "I Am Strong." My father was so excited about the message. He lifted his hands and said, "I am Strong!"

I was so happy he was home with Chris and me! "I can now take care of my daddy." I said to myself.

After bathing, my father felt much better and went right to sleep.

My father was with me for 7 days! During this time, he wasn't eating much, and he was vomiting.

One particular night, he realized he was vomiting his bowels, so I rushed him to the hospital. They admitted him right away.

He told me, "Leave me here in hospice. I don't want to die in your house where you and my grandson have to live."

I did not want to leave him, but I had to go pick up the kids. By the time I made it home, I got a call from the hospital telling me that my father had passed away.

My hero! My first love! My *e-ve-ry-thing* has left this earth!

I had to find a way to honor the man and father he was. So, I wrote a tribute for my father and shared it at his homegoing service:

I Remember Daddy

As I end this journey down memory lane and remembering my daddy in his final days, they wasn't the prettiest, they wasn't the easiest I'm sad to say. But I thought I would try something to see what he'd say. I sniffed his beard and asked, "Daddy, what's that smell?" He smiled. "What does it smell like?" he replied. Shocked that he remembered, I paused and couldn't talk and turned away. If you were here and asked me now Daddy, I'd reply and say, "You smell like a Man who has stood strong throughout the years...a Man that has been sober for over 18 years. You smell like a laborer who worked until he could work no more...a friend who always kept an open door...a friend who cracked jokes, listened to music, and played cards...an over-protective skinny brother who swore he was hard!...a father who took great care of his kids...a Grandfather that saw no wrong no matter what his grandkids did...a Father that demanded of a man to come to him first before asking for his daughter's hand...a Daddy who smells like a white dove flying free on the sunniest of days...there's only one you and I will always remember YOU in a happy way!

After everything had calmed down, I couldn't wait to feel close to my father again. So, I went to collect all of my father's music and equipment about 2 days after the funeral. But his wife had given ALL 903 of his CD's (*purposely*) to her cousin and wouldn't give them back. This evil act made me feel like my father died all over again. Her mission was accomplished: She wanted to hurt me, and she hurt me deeply.

I took on the request of my father to care for my 3 younger siblings ages 9, 11 and 15. So, suddenly I'm a parent of 4 and a soon-to-be graduate with a bachelor's degree in Christian ministries and organizational leadership.

Damone and I were able to co-parent well. Christian was now spending more time with his father's side of the family and meeting, his older brothers and sisters.

RISE ABOVE THE ORDINARY: The Life Behind Her Smile

Afterward, I remember Christian coming home excited that he wasn't the only child.

He always raved about his grandmother named Candy.

Damone was an excellent father to his children; Damone and his children had a bond no one could break. He taught Chris and his other brothers about legacy and ancestry, and where they come from as black young kings. He taught them to "always take care of your mother, do what your big brother says, and be a good example for your little brothers." He *drilled* this into them, and he was serious about it! He showed them toughness, his vulnerable side, and the love of a father.

In April of 2016, my and my son's life was shaken to the core as I woke up to a phone call from one of Christian's brother's mother (Shimmy) screaming, "Damone was killed!!"

I have never felt so lost for words!

Hearing that the father of my child, my best friend, my protector, my safe space has died, a piece of me died with him.

He had given up a lot and changed so much to be a greater person for his children and grandchildren! "Why now?" is what I was left with.

He was so much to *so* many people!

He was my Clyde, and he has left us all for good! His children will never be the same.

I was met with many challenges in this situation of taking in my siblings, but I did what I do best… I prayed and I prevailed as I always have. I rose above the rough streets of life. But there are so many children and adults who didn't make it through their wilderness; this is why I'm forever thankful and humble and careful not to put my mouth on other people: I know that, *even* though the life behind Lakisha's smile was bad, there's still someone else who was worse off than her. Be grateful!

And Finally My Brethren

Life brought many challenges for my family, especially my mom and all 8 of her children.

RISE ABOVE THE ORDINARY: The Life Behind Her Smile

Contrary to what it looked like and what most people in our situation would have turned out to be my siblings and I have become the epitome of what it looks like to *Rise Above The Ordinary*:

All of my mother's children graduated from high school.

Donnell (Boona) is a supportive father of 4.
Falisha is a fantastic mother of 2 and owns and operates a successful daycare.
Michael married the love of his life and is gainfully employed.
Stephanie went to Culinary school where she met her husband Lavelle. She's been married 18 years now and has 3 sons. She also works as my sou chef.
Nikki is a mother of 2 and currently working her career job for the past 17 years.
Verlene is the store manager in the Restaurant industry.
Steve was married 5 years before he died in his sleep 10 years ago.

Our brother's death shook our family hard. He is the missing link to our 8-piece puzzle.

LAKISHA P HUNTER

We are all in church and proud Members of The Powerhouse Chicago Church (formally PFOM), where I have been a member and Ordained Elder for 21 years, under the leadership of Archbishop William Hudson III and Pastor Andria Hudson.

I am the 2nd eldest of my mother's 8 children, and I do my best to lead by example.

I am a former *Ward of the State* and gang member who had a learning disability and is now looking to make a difference for those just like me and my family.

I am a graduate of Trinity International University with a master's degree in urban ministries.

I am the founder of RATO, a nonprofit organization and mentorship program that serves youth and young adults and those re-entering society.

I have been in the restaurant industry for 30 years, and I'm the owner of *That Jerk Spot* a mobile food truck company.

I have 3 amazing sons - my love child Christian (17) and my joy child Kaden (7), and my bonus son Jalen (21).

In 2014, I finally made it to the altar and got married. We had the most beautiful, *fairytale* wedding.

But no one ever tells you the truth about *The Life Behind The Ring*!

Langston Hughes said it best: "...Life for me ain't been no crystal stair."

But I can do all things through Christ that strengthens me.

He does all things WELL!...No Mistake.

LAKISHA P HUNTER

DEDICATION

RISE ABOVE THE ORDINARY: The Life Behind Her Smile

I dedicate "*The Life Behind Her Smile*" in loving memory of my mother,
Rochelle Petrice Hunter.

Mom, the life behind your smile wasn't all peaches and cream, yet you took the lemons that you had and made lemonade: your children. You gave birth to 8 children when you could have chosen differently.

Yeah, you broke a lot of rules in life, LOL, but in the end, you made up for a lot of them.

You were able to do something I have yet to conquer you lived life on your *own* terms, which, as an adult, I see is much harder to do.

Looking back, I see that you were stronger than anyone had given you credit for. Strong because even when you would do so so good, evil was always present to remind you of what life had dealt to you at such a young age, yet you bounced back in spite of the odds. Through it all you laughed, you kept your sense of humor, My God you were hilarious with the jokes! LOL!

You won, girl! From your bedside I watched you fight 'til the end was over, and you took your last breath. You won the battle because you received forgiveness from your children. Your life has taught me that it's not always about how you start out, but how you finish. You have finished well, grasshopper…you finished well! Therefore, you left this earth with what you deserved most: LOVE.

I love you, but God loved you best.

THANK YOU

RISE ABOVE THE ORDINARY: The Life Behind Her Smile

Teachers are to be the guide, empowering, encouraging leaders and living examples for students to look up to. John Hope Community Academy had the best examples of this definition: Mrs. D.W Robinson, Fran Robinson, Mrs. C. Jackson, and Mrs. C. Walker (RIP).

***

Englewood High School Eagles Flies High because of these beautiful souls pushing me to soar: Darlene Austin, Judith Hayes, Doris Brown, Charles Pugh, Mr. Vabornick, James Lampkin, Gwen Miller (RIP), Dr. Paulette Kidd (RIP), Barbra Johnson (BJ), Desiree Mathis, Mrs. Mary Jackson, Mrs. Mary Smith, and Coach Richard Henderson. I thank you all ♥ saving my life.

***

To Mrs. Darlene Austin, thank you for saving my life and for broadening my horizons. I am who I am as a businesswoman because of that initial pour. Thank you for the motherly love you've given me. I pray God grants you the desires of your heart. I will always love you for the push and the patience in all the pushback I'd given in my transitions of life.

LAKISHA P HUNTER

To my "Daily," my father away from my father. Walking me down the aisle in my father's stead still holds solid in my heart. I love you for who you are and how you made me feel like your daughter. My brothers from another mother, Rick Austin, and Lamar Austin. You two loved me from day 1. You've supported and given me advice as the overprotective brother you are. Thank you for the small talk and heavy ones too! Thanks for having my back ALWAYS!!

***

I truly thank God for the community that God has blessed me with! In making the transition into a new church and then becoming pregnant while in training in ministry, the support and encouragement to endure was 2nd to none. You all made sure I would not fall into a depressed state for the shame and embarrassment: Paula Dickens, EmDee, Lamekia Davis, Anita Thomas, Samone Boyd, Tamara Goshay, Donna Booker, Catherine, McNeil, Crystal Turner. Thank you. I love my village.

***

Que Payne, Jolene Taylor, Allyson Vaux, Greg Thomas, Fran Thomas, Creola Hampton, Deborah Lane, and Pastor Deirdre and Apostle Kevin Cunningham, thank you for being that supportive force and that encouraging voice. You all are my safety net and I thank God for who you are individually in my life.

***

My Spiritual Leaders: Archbishop William Hudson III, you have handled me gracefully and carefully as your spiritual daughter. You made room for me to be open and honest without judgement. Thank you also for the charge and the push! And Pastor Andria Hudson, aka My "HOMIE," you've come at the right time in my life. I wrote this story in 2009 and shared it with you then, and MY God! In 2024 it's unfolding into this beautiful piece of reading. You've spoken multiple things into my life and God has brought His word to pass. You're a true gift to me spiritually and personally.

RISE ABOVE THE ORDINARY: The Life Behind Her Smile

www.ingramcontent.com/pod-product-compliance
Lightning Source LLC
Chambersburg PA
CBHW050128170426
43197CB00011B/1756